EFFECTIVE PRACTICE IN THE EARLY YEARS

PANSY MCFARLANE-EDMOND
CHRISTINE WITHERS

EFFECTIVE PRACTICE IN THE EARLY YEARS

Learning Matters,
A SAGE Publishing Company
1 Oliver's Yard
55 City Road
London EC1Y 1SP

SAGE Publications Inc.
2455 Teller Road
Thousand Oaks, California 91320

SAGE Publications India Pvt Ltd
B 1/I 1 Mohan Cooperative Industrial Area
Mathura Road
New Delhi 110 044

SAGE Publications Asia-Pacific Pte Ltd
3 Church Street
#10-04 Samsung Hub
Singapore 049483

Library of Congress Control Number: 2023930606

British Library Cataloguing in Publication Data

A catalogue record for this book is available from the British Library

Editor: Amy Thornton
Senior project editor: Chris Marke
Cover design: Wendy Scott
Typeset by: TNQ Technologies
Printed in the UK

ISBN 978-1-5297-9884-5
ISBN 978-1-5297-9883-8 (pbk)

Contents

Acknowledgements

Pansy

I would like to thank my husband, Peter, and my daughters, Gemma and Hope, for their continual love and support. With gratitude to my parents Mavis and Edward (Eddie) McFarlane who were part of the Windrush generation, I wish to dedicate this book to them.

I would also like to thank Christine, my co-writer, for the great working relationship developed during this book writing journey.

Christine

My heartfelt thanks go to my family and my husband Kevin who have supported me to follow my passion for Early Years throughout. I have been inspired by my children George, Zoe, Claire and Morgan and am grateful for the families and children, students and colleagues I have had the pleasure to learn from. I would like thank Pansy for her great teamwork and commitment to realise this book.

We would like to thank our colleague, Berhane Dory, for sharing initial ideas and expertise and for her encouragement throughout the project.

About the Authors

Pansy McFarlane-Edmond of Black British African-Caribbean heritage is a Senior Lecturer in Early Childhood Studies at the London Metropolitan University. She teaches on both undergraduate and postgraduate programmes which includes a practice based module. She has over 40 years experience working within the Early Years field, including 20 years combined experience teaching in both Further and Higher Education. Her experience includes working closely with children and their families, assessing students, and leading and managing practice within a range of settings (nursery class, day nurseries, Children and Families LA, a Sure Start Local Programme and Children Centres).

Pansy holds additional responsibilities at the London Metropolitan University within the School of Social Sciences and Professions which includes Departmental Safety Liaison Officer, Academic Liaison Tutor (working in partnership with colleges in the United Kingdom and abroad) and is an external examiner for a university and college outside of London.

Her recent collaborative research publication includes '*An evaluation of the experience of the hidden curriculum of Black and minority ethnic undergraduate health and safety social care students at a London University*' (*Journal of Further and Higher Education*, 2021).

Christine Withers is a Senior Lecturer in Early Childhood Studies at London Metropolitan University. She leads and teaches on a range of modules at the undergraduate and postgraduate levels including practice-based modules, and assesses students in placement. As part of her teaching role, Christine supported students achieving Graduate Practitioner Competencies and supports students on the distance learning programme of the early childhood studies programme. Christine brings to her teaching over 25 years of experience working in a range of settings across the early childhood sector in England such as play groups, day nurseries, and through voluntary engagement in a Sure Start Children Centre and in reception classes. She held leadership roles in a Steiner Waldorf early childhood setting and a day nursery. Subsequent to gaining Early Years Professional Status (EYPS), she has mentored and assessed EYPS candidates.

Introduction

A child's experience in the early years has a major impact on their future life chances.

(Department for Children, Schools and Families, 2008, p7)

There are numerous definitions for what effective practice within the Early Years (EY) is and looks like. Within the context of this book, it is about ensuring that all children as well as staff are enabled and given the best opportunities to develop and progress. It is also concerned with supporting children to gain full access to the curriculum and for children and staff to attain their potential and get the most out of their experience within the setting. It is important that we provide the best for every child including high-quality care (Grenier, 2020). Effective practice is closely aligned to what is considered as best practice. Throughout the book we will consider what this looks like at various points. Examples from research (e.g., Sylva et al., 2004) will be linked to practice, and reflective tasks will be used to support you, the reader in gaining a deeper understanding of what effective practice involves.

The idea for this book emerged from our experience of teaching practice-based modules as part of the Early Childhood Studies degree course at London Metropolitan University. These practice modules support students to achieve the level three Early Years Educator (EYE) qualification (Department for Education, 2019) in addition to their undergraduate degree. The EYE qualification allows students working in the EY sector to be counted in the ratio of staff and children, offering better prospects of employment and potential for further professional development (Department for Education, 2019). Students who continue their professional practice journey at level six of the degree are often working towards the award of Early Childhood Graduate Practitioner (The Quality Assurance Agency for Higher Education (QAA), 2022). The respective qualifications are integral to their degree award.

We are passionate about delivering learning and teaching in the subject area of Early Childhood Studies which is enriched by students' practice and lived experiences and their reflections. Therefore, we envisaged a publication that addresses what effective practice in EY may look like. This book speaks to all stakeholders involved in the student journey and will be essential to those involved in supporting students to gain a recognised EY practice qualification. We focus on babies and young children between the age range of 0–8, and therefore will cover areas of the Early Years Foundation Stage (DfE, 2021a) and the National Curriculum (DfE, 2013).

As discussed above, this book is for a range of professionals and stakeholders who have an interest in developing or supporting effective practice. It is intended to support and guide students with their written work and relevant assessments and aims to link closely to theory and practice. It is also a valuable guide for tutors who support students on a range of degree programmes. This includes those who are assessed or who need underpinning knowledge and understanding of effective practice within EY. As you read through, you will notice that a number of chapters include relevant case studies, reflective tasks, and provide examples where necessary to support different learning styles and to enhance and support deeper knowledge and understanding of practice. We recommend using a reflective journal as you engage with the tasks and activities. Chapter 9 explains what a reflective journal is and how to use it.

Underpinning values for Early Years practice

This book is underpinned by the EY values we expect to be upheld when working with young children, their families and other professionals. Values are the things that we see as important such as the need to be child focussed and always acting in the best interest of the child (Unicef, 1989). Embracing diversity in the broadest sense and being inclusive is essential and another core value of EY practice. These values must always be at the heart of provision. You will see that the book conveys an atmosphere within settings of mutual respect, the need to build positive relationships and the importance of the meeting children's individual needs while working in partnership with parents and families (DfE, 2021a). Bronfenbrenner (1979) discusses the relevance of the home and setting environment as well as positive relationships between both impacting favourably on children's outcomes. The book will, therefore, give emphasis to working in partnership with parents and professionals.

Historical, social and political context of Early Years provision

This section aims to provide the reader with a historical overview and a broad timeline of how EY provision and practice have developed. Based on our understanding Early Childhood Education and Care (ECEC) being located within a broad social and political context, we offer a brief historical foundation of EY provision in the United Kingdom. The beginnings of early childhood provision are explored to understand practice and provision in EY and education settings within its current social and political context.

Early Childhood Education (ECE) in the United Kingdom goes back just over 200 years when in 1816 Robert Owen (1771–1858) founded the first nursery school in New Lanark in Scotland for children of cotton mill workers. He created provision for children aged 1 to 6 years old that favoured informal teaching and physical activities. Owen's ideas were ahead of his time and led to an interest in ECE and establishment of infant schools in Britain (Young-Ihm, 2002). These new ideas emerged from a social context that saw children generally as labourers. Legislation such as the Factory Act 1833 paved the way to offer some protection for children from child labour, and the increasing mechanisation in industry resulted in fewer children being needed as labourers (UK Parliament, 2022a). The Education Act 1870 was the first piece of legislation created to deal specifically with the provision of education in Britain. The Education Act 1880 finally made school attendance compulsory between the ages of five and ten (UK Parliament, 2022b).

A milestone in the development of EY provision was a report for the Education board in 1905, which highlighted a lack of suitable provision for young children and made a recommendation for separate facilities for children under five. It was not long after, that the importance of proper nourishment and health care for young children was advocated by Margaret McMillan (1860–1931) and her sister Rachel. They established an open-air nursery for poor children in Deptford in 1911, where children were free to play outdoors, and children's health and well-being was prioritised (Giardiello, 2014). The establishment of a teacher training college in 1930 was a further legacy of Margaret McMillan (Giardiello, 2014). The Hadow report (1933, pp108, 187, in Gillard, 2006) recognised that education in nursery schools has 'value of its own as an educational instrument' and should be provided particularly 'in districts where the housing and general economic conditions are seriously below the average'. The need for training for those working in nursery provision became pressing in the 1940s when the demand for childcare provision rose during the Second World War. Local Education Authorities (LEA's) were charged with the provision of training for those working in nursery schools offering programmes such as the National Society of Day Nurseries (NSDN) diploma. In 1945, the birth of the National Nursery Examination Board (NNEB) gained recognition as appropriate training for young women in Further Education (FE) colleges. The value of early education by government was further strengthened with the Nursery and Childminder Regulation Act 1948, which required provisions for under 5's to be registered with the local authority. Due to lack of funding nursery school provision was limited, and only with the advent of the pre-school playgroup movement in 1961 part-time provision for children became more widely available and welcomed as an alternative to nursery schools (Young-Ihm, 2002). The NNEB eventually merged with the Council for Early Years Awards (CEYA) to form the Council for Awards in Care, Health and Education (CACHE) in 1994.

When the Labour government came into power in 1997, they had a clear commitment and focus on reducing the number of children living in poverty. This led to the development of national policies and initiatives such as the National Childcare Strategy in 1998 with the aim of developing quality EY childcare provision enabling parents to enter the labour market (Nursery World, 2001). This development coincided with the emergence of terminology such as 'effective pedagogy' as a quality indicator relating to the EY sector. Large studies considered the impact ECE on outcomes for children, namely the effective provision of pre-school education (EPPE) project (Sylva et al., 2004) and the study researching effective pedagogy in the early years (REPEY) (Siraj-Blatchford et al., 2002). Both these studies paved the way for further policy development impacting on the qualification levels within the EY sector. This led to government funding being made available to ensure the development of graduate level practitioners in EY.

Practitioners educated to NVQ level 3 were able to access university degree courses such as early childhood studies undergraduate degree programmes and enter the sector as graduate leaders (Fitzgerald and Kay, 2016). This policy development aimed to professionalise the EY workforce in the hope of achieving positive long-term outcomes for children and their families, particularly those who come from disadvantaged backgrounds (Allen, 2011; Field, 2010).

The Childcare Act 2006 paved the way for the first statutory guidance 'Setting the Standards for Learning, Development and Care for children from birth to five' (DCSF, 2008, p1). A clear commitment from the government towards high-quality childcare and the resulting need for highly qualified staff was met with the intro-duction of the Early Years Professional Status (EYPS), a higher education qualifi-cation at level 6 first established in 2007 by the Children's Workforce Development Council (CWDC, 2008a).

Further changes to EY graduate qualifications were introduced, such as the Early Years Teacher Status in 2013, the post-graduate qualification of Early Years Teacher. In addition, the Early Childhood Graduate Practitioner Competencies were integrated into the QAA Subject Benchmark Statement for Early Childhood Studies (QAA, 2022); these developments showed a continued commitment towards a highly educated early childhood sector.

How the book is organised

The ten chapters (including this introductory chapter) of this book have been designed to give increased flexibility for its use, allowing you to explore chapters that are relevant to discussions, particular subject matters or the course you are undertaking. It does not need to be read in order and below we have outlined briefly what you may expect from each chapter:

Chapter 1 considers Perspectives on Children's Rights and examines the history of the United Nations Conventions on the Rights of the Child (UNCRC) (Unicef, 1989) and its implementation in relation to sociological perspectives of children and childhood. It highlights how these rights are enshrined in English law and the impact it has on practice within different EY contexts.

This chapter links to the relevant criteria for:

Early Years Educator (Department for Education and National College for Teaching and Leadership, 2019).

- 1. Support and promote children's early education and development

- 4. Develop effective and informed practice

(Continued)

(Continued)

Early Childhood Graduate Practitioner (Early Childhood Studies Degree Network, 2019).

- Competency 1 – Advocating for young children's rights and participation
- Competency 3 – Work directly with young children, families and colleagues to promote health, well-being, safety and nurturing care
- Competency 4 – Observe, listen and plan for young children to support their well-being, early learning, progression and transition
- Competency 6 – Inclusive practice
- Competency 9 – Professional development

Chapter 2 explores The Impact of Legislation and Policies on Provision and Practice. We consider the historical perspectives of UK legislation and policies on provision within a UK context. The importance of these and the impact they have on policies, provision, practice, children, families and relevant stakeholders are discussed.

This chapter links to the relevant criteria for:

Early Years Educator (Department for Education and National College for Teaching and Leadership, 2019).

- 1. Support and promote children's early education and development
- 5. Safeguard and promote the health, safety and welfare of children

Early Childhood Graduate Practitioner (Early Childhood Studies Degree Network, 2019).

- Competency 3 – Work directly with young children, families and colleagues to promote health, well-being, safety and nurturing care
- Competency 5 – Safeguarding and child protection
- Competency 9 – Professional development

Chapter 3 reflects on how we work with Diverse Families and relevant Professionals to support children's well-being. It explores perspectives on what diverse families may look like and the role of a range of professionals within EY. It considers the challenges and barriers to effective partnership working.

This chapter links to the relevant criteria for:

Early Years Educator (Department for Education and National College for Teaching and Leadership, 2019).

- 1. Support and promote children's early education and development
- 2. Plan and provide effective care, teaching and learning that enables children to progress and prepares them for school
- 3. Make accurate and productive use of assessment
- 6. Work in partnership with the key person, colleagues, parents and/or carers or other professionals

Early Childhood Graduate Practitioner (Early Childhood Studies Degree Network, 2019).

- Competency 7 – Partnership with parents and caregivers

Chapter 4 looks at Leading Practice and explores how EY practitioners can be empowered in their knowledge and skills to lead within a range of EY contexts. It explores the importance of working within and supporting teams.

This chapter links to the relevant criteria for:

Early Years Educator (Department for Education and National College for Teaching and Leadership, 2019).

- 4. Develop effective and informed practice
- 5. Safeguard and promote the health, safety and welfare of children
- 6. Work in partnership with the key person, colleagues, parents and/or carers or other professionals

Early Childhood Graduate Practitioner (Early Childhood Studies Degree Network, 2019).

- Competency 3 – Work directly with young children, families and colleagues to promote health, well-being, safety and nurturing care
- Competency 4 – Observe, listen and plan for young children to support their well-being, early learning, progression and transition

(Continued)

(Continued)

- Competency 5 – Safeguarding and child protection
- Competency 6 – Inclusive practice
- Competency 7 – Partnership with parents and caregivers
- Competency 8 – Collaborating with others
- Competency 9 – Professional development

Chapter 5 discusses Effective Safeguarding. It offers insight into the scope of safeguarding in early childhood practice, and for the reader to gain an awareness of safeguarding processes in EY settings. It considers how to promote children's welfare, the role of the student, practitioner, and other professionals in relation to safeguarding procedures and working with statutory agencies.

This chapter links to the relevant criteria for:

Early Years Educator (Department for Education and National College for Teaching and Leadership, 2019).

- 2. Plan and provide effective care, teaching and learning that enables children to progress and prepares them for school
- 5. Safeguard and promote the health, safety and welfare of children
- 6. Work in partnership with the key person, colleagues, parents and/or carers or other professionals

Early Childhood Graduate Practitioner (Early Childhood Studies Degree Network, 2019).

- Competency 5 – Safeguarding and child protection
- Competency 7 – Partnership with parents and caregivers
- Competency 8 – Collaborating with others
- Competency 9 – Professional development

Chapter 6 explores the Importance of Assessed Practice. This chapter guides the reader through the placement journey and aims to encourage those in placement practice to reflect on their learning and experiences using a reflective learning journal. The importance of developing positive relationships within the setting and embracing core professional values and the impact this has on practice is shown. Practical guidance will support students and practitioners through their practice assessments and the important role of the mentor and visiting tutor is explained.

This chapter links to the relevant criteria for:

Early Years Educator (Department for Education and National College for Teaching and Leadership, 2019).

- 1. Support and promote children's early education and development
- 4. Develop effective and informed practice
- 5. Safeguard and promote the health, safety and welfare of children
- 6. Work in partnership with the key person, colleagues, parents and/or carers or other professionals

Early Childhood Graduate Practitioner (Early Childhood Studies Degree Network, 2019).

- Competency 1 – Advocating for young children's rights and participation
- Competency 4 – Observe, listen and plan for young children to support their well-being, early learning, progression and transition
- Competency 7 – Partnership with parents and caregivers
- Competency 8 – Collaborating with others

Chapter 7 looks at Assessment within the Early Years Foundation Stage (EYFS) and Key Stage 1 (KS1). It introduces the reader to concepts of assessment within EYFS and KS1 highlighting the importance of observation to inform the planning cycle. Students and practitioners are guided to develop effective planning within their setting. Documentation of Learning is considered as a meaningful alternative assessment. Discussions involving statutory aspects of assessment within the EYFS and KS1 will support the reader in developing their practice in a critically reflective way.

This chapter links to the relevant criteria for:

Early Years Educator (Department for Education and National College for Teaching and Leadership, 2019).

- 1. Support and promote children's early education and development
- 3. Make accurate and productive use of assessment

(Continued)

(Continued)

- 6. Work in partnership with the key person, colleagues, parents and/or carers or other professionals

Early Childhood Graduate Practitioner (Early Childhood Studies Degree Network, 2019).

- Competency 1 – Advocating for young children's rights and participation
- Competency 4 – Observe, listen and plan for young children to support their well-being, early learning, progression and transition
- Competency 6 – Inclusive practice
- Competency 7 – Partnership with parents and caregivers

Chapter 8 explores Inclusive Practice and aims to promote an inclusive approach to EY practice founded on the values and principles of education for social justice. Using case studies, together with integration of current policy contexts, this chapter explores how an inclusive approach can be realised in EY settings. It discusses some of the challenges or barriers to inclusive practice and considers how students and practitioners in placement can support and promote inclusive practice more effectively.

This chapter links to the relevant criteria for:

Early Years Educator (Department for Education and National College for Teaching and Leadership, 2019).

- 2. Plan and provide effective care, teaching and learning that enables children to progress and prepares them for school
- 6. Work in partnership with the key person, colleagues, parents and/or carers or other professionals

Early Childhood Graduate Practitioner (Early Childhood Studies Degree Network, 2019).

- Competency 1 – Advocating for young children's rights and participation
- Competency 6 – Inclusive practice

Chapter 9 is the final chapter which looks at the importance of **Continuous Professional Development and Next Steps**. It considers why lifelong learning and continuous professional development is seen as integral to being an effective EY practitioner. It supports students as well as practitioners to set targets and helps them to plan and identify possible professional development pathways.

This chapter links to the relevant criteria for:

Early Years Educator (Department for Education and National College for Teaching and Leadership, 2019).

- 4. Develop effective and informed practice

Early Childhood Graduate Practitioner (Early Childhood Studies Degree Network, 2019).

- Competency 9 – Professional development

1   Perspectives on children's rights

I believe we should claim certain rights for the children and labour for their universal recognition...

Eglantyne Jebb (Forsyth, 2013)

Why is knowledge and understanding of children's rights important for practitioners and how may this impact on their practice?

Students and practitioners who are participating within the community of the early childhood setting and are in direct interaction with children and their families should have a good understanding of children's rights (Unicef, 1989) which can help guide their practice. Practitioners who are knowledgeable in this area are best equipped to support and implement a children's rights approach within their practice. As can be seen below, the criteria for the Early Years Educator as well as the Early Childhood Graduate Practitioner are informed by the viewpoint that promoting children's rights in early childhood practice is integral to the role of the practitioner. Reflective practitioners who understand the contexts in which children's rights can flourish are guided by the values and principles of inclusion and social justice, which this chapter will further explore.

CHAPTER OVERVIEW

In this chapter we aim to help you develop your understanding of:

- Sociological perspectives of children and childhood
- The history of the United Nations Convention on the Rights of the Child (Unicef, 1989)
- Children's Rights in the context of UK legislation
- How to support children's rights in early childhood settings

---

You will find that Chapters 2, 3, 4, 7 and 8 link closely to the topics discussed within this chapter.

This chapter links to the relevant criteria for:

Early Years Educator (Department for Education and National College for Teaching and Leadership, 2019)

- 1.3 Understand a range of underpinning theories and philosophical approaches to how children learn and develop and their influence on practice;

- 1.5 Understand the importance of promoting diversity, equality and inclusion, fully reflecting cultural differences and family circumstances;

- 1.8 Understand the potential effects of, and how to prepare and support children through, transitions and significant events in their lives;

- 1.10 Promote equality of opportunity and anti-discriminatory practice;

- 4.3 Engage in continuing professional development and reflective practice to improve own skills, practice and subject knowledge

Early Childhood Graduate Practitioner Competencies (Early Childhood Studies Degree Network, 2019).

- 1.1 Demonstrate how you listen to and work in collaboration with young children, individually and in groups;

- 1.2 Observe, support and extend young children's participation in their learning through following their needs and interests;

- 1.3 Support children to respect others by providing opportunities for their participation and decision making;

- 3.3 Apply data protection legislation to practice;

- 3.6 Demonstrate the application of knowledge and understanding about the importance of respectful nurturing care routines;

- 4.4 Apply theoretical understanding to the range of transitions young children experience and how these can be supported in practice;

- 6.1 Evidence knowledge, understanding and application in practice of pedagogy that supports inclusion;

(Continued)

(Continued)

- 9.1 Demonstrate self-awareness and knowledge of anti-discriminatory practice, promoting social justice and the importance of valuing difference;

- 9.4 Draw on research to demonstrate knowledge of leadership and management and its importance and application in democratic and inclusive practice.

Who is considered a child and how can we understand childhood from a sociological perspective?

According to the United Nations Conventions on the Rights of the Child (UNCRC) (Unicef, 1989), a child is 'any human being below the age of eighteen years unless under the law applicable to the child, majority is attained earlier'. Age determines whether a person is considered as a child, and it follows that granting children's rights in line with this UN international treaty is dependent on a specific political and societal context. The rich diversity of these contexts across the globe not only shape children's experience of childhood but also the rights and responsibilities afforded to them. James and Prout (2015) made a valuable contribution to our understanding of childhood. They distinguished between the immaturity of children, which they consider as a biological fact of life, and how this immaturity is perceived across time, socio-cultural and political contexts. This led them to affirm the notion of childhood as a social construction. It is this understanding of childhood, which informs this chapter and demands as Burr (2015, p2) suggests 'that we take a critical stance toward our taken-for-granted ways of understanding the world and ourselves' and remove ourselves from the idea of childhood as universally experienced.

In the West, the advent of Enlightenment brought Rousseau's (1712–1778) ideas to the fore and the view of the child as innately good, innocent and in need of protection (Clark, 2010). In the twentieth century, the recognition of childhood as a developmental stage led not only to an understanding of children's needs as distinct to those of adults but inferred the notion of the child as lacking when compared to adults. This view goes hand in hand with the separation of the child's world from that of the adult and is visible in the way many societies and their institutions are organised (Archard, 2015). In addition, childhood as a distinct area of social research is integral to the way childhood is understood in the West today. The notion of children as rights holders is well established today and anchored within the international human rights treaty, the UNCRC (Unicef, 1989). This treaty sets out the civil, political, economic, social and cultural rights of every child, regardless of their race, religion or abilities. However, when attributing children with rights specific to their needs, the presumption of western ideals may overlook the lived experience of children across different political and socio-cultural contexts (Archard, 2015). For example, child labour is part of children's experience in some countries, where children are contributing to the labour market and family's income (Wells, 2015).

The development of children's rights

'The Declaration of the Rights of the Child' was first drafted by Eglantyne Jebb (1876–1928) in 1923 and is seen as her greatest achievement. The activist's campaigning work included fundraising for children who were suffering famine at the end of the First World War in 1918, by setting up 'The Save the Children Fund' in 1919, which formed the basis of the charity we know today (Forsyth, 2013). The declaration was endorsed by the League of Nations the following year and became the foundation of the UNCRC (Unicef, 1989). The 'Geneva Declaration of the Rights of the Child' recognised for the first time that children are rights holders and that it is the responsibility of adults to ensure children are materially and spiritually supported, fed and sheltered, and protected from exploitation.

In 1945, at the end of the Second World War, the international community recognised the need for a joint statement of human rights, and when in 1948, 54 member states of the United Nations (UN) agreed to the Universal Declaration of Human Rights, the rights and freedoms for 'all peoples and all nations' were presented in this historic document (UN, 2022, p1). While the Universal Declaration of Human Rights (UN, 2022, p7) recognised 'motherhood and childhood are entitled to special care and assistance', it was not seen to safeguard the specific rights of children. In 1959, the UN General Assembly adopted the Declaration on the Rights of the Child, which were then 10 principles. When the United Nations Assembly declared 1979 as the Year of the Child, and its commission on Human Rights set out to establish a working group to develop a draft convention, the UNCRC (Unicef, 1989) as we know it today was created. It took another 10 years for the working group to present it before the UN General Assembly, and the Convention was adopted on 20 November 1989, the 30th anniversary of the Declaration on the Rights of the Child.

All UN member states with exception of the United States of America have ratified the UNCRC (Unicef, 2022). The United Kingdom ratified the Convention on 16 December 1991, and as international law the treaty should be taken account of when decisions are made that affect children. The fact that a country has ratified the Convention does not ensure that children's rights are necessarily respected and realised, for this to happen they would need to be made part of the domestic law. In England, for example, children cannot go to court relying solely on the UNCRC (Children's Rights Alliance for England, 2022). However, with the adoption of Human Rights into UK law, there is an expectation by the European Court of Human Rights that national authorities 'treat the best interests of a child as a "primary consideration"' (UK Parliament, 2015). Further, the United Nations Committee on the Rights of the Child oversees the implementation of the UNCRC. This means that every 5 years governments are examined on how well they are progressing in implementing the UN Convention on the Rights of the Child and recommendations to governments are made. Although the UNCRC is the treaty protecting the rights of children which most countries have agreed on, there are other Conventions that have been ratified by numerous states. To widen your perspective, you may want to look at the African Charter on the Rights and Welfare of the Child, adopted on 1 July 1990 by the African Union (then Organisation of African Unity) within a year of the United Nations adopting the Convention on the Rights of the Child. The African Charter on the Rights and Welfare of the Child came into force in 1999 and has been ratified by 49 African countries so far (African Union, 2019).

The United Nations Convention on the Rights of the Child (UNCRC) (Unicef, 1989)

The UNCRC is anchored on four articles, which set out the 'General Principles' (Unicef, 2022) of the Convention and which support the interpretation of all articles within the UNCRC. These principles are:

- Non-discrimination (article 2)

  - This is expressed in article 2 and ensures the rights as articulated in the UNCRC apply to all children 'without discrimination of any kind'.

- Best interest of the child (article 3)

  - Article 3 outlines that 'in all actions concerning children, whether undertaken by public or private social welfare institutions, courts of law, administrative authorities or legislative bodies, the best interests of the child shall be a primary consideration'.

- Right to life, survival and development (article 6)

  - Within article 6 is enshrined that 'every child has the inherent right to life' and that 'States Parties shall ensure to the maximum extent possible the survival and development of the child'.

- Right to be heard (article 12)

  - Article 12 lays out the right of 'the child who is capable of forming his or her own views to express those views freely in all matters affecting the child' and 'that the views of the child being given due weight in accordance with the age and maturity of the child'.

(Unicef, 1989, pp3, 4)

In its 54 articles, the Convention set out the rights of all children, everywhere and these encompass all areas of a child's life (Unicef, 2022). These areas embrace children's economic, social, cultural, civil and political rights (Jones, 2011). Optional protocols expand children's rights specifically regarding the involvement of children in armed conflict, the sale of children, child prostitution and child pornography. Further, they extend to the right of the child to be able to challenge violations of their rights outside their legal justice system and bring a complaint to the United Nations. Optional protocols do not have to be accepted by countries that have ratified the UNCRC.

In articles 43 to 54, the UNCRC (Unicef, 1989) sets out the responsibilities of adults and governments to ensure these rights are upheld. The convention refers also to the responsibilities of children in relation to their rights. Article 29 states that the education of the child 'shall be directed to the development of respect for human rights and fundamental freedoms, and for the principles enshrined in the Charter of the United Nations' and also the 'development of respect for the natural environment' (Unicef, 1989, p9). This means that children need to respect each other's rights. Further, if children have a right to a clean environment, then they also have a responsibility to do what they can to look after the environment. You may note that the African Charter on the Rights and Welfare of the Child attributes responsibilities also to the child regarding his family, society, the state and the international community. As outlined in article 31 of the African charter on the Rights and Welfare of the Child such responsibilities include, for example, to strive for the unity of the family, show respect to parents, superiors and elders and support them when necessary and to be of service to their national community physically and intellectually (African Union, 1990).

Reflective task

Visit the Unicef website to download the UNCRC. Read the articles that entail the General Principles of the UNCRC (Unicef, 1989) and reflect on the following questions:

- Why is the UNCRC important for EY practitioners and in early childhood practice?

- How are the principles of the UNCRC respected in your practice?

- How are children informed about their rights within your setting?

Read through all the articles (for this task, you can access the summary document online):

- Are there any articles you are surprised by, and if so, why?

Moving from a needs-based perspective to a children's right's perspective

The rights of the child as stated by the UNCRC (Unicef, 1989) are commonly grouped into different types of rights. Save the Children (2016) differentiate these rights into the following themes:

Survival rights

These rights include the child's right to life and the needs that are most basic to existence, such as nutrition, shelter, an adequate living standard, health and access to medical services.

Development rights

These rights encompass the right to education, play, leisure, cultural activities, access to information and freedom of thought, conscience and religion.

Protection rights

These rights ensure children are safeguarded against all forms of abuse, neglect and exploitation, including special care for refugee children; safeguards for children in the criminal justice system; protection for children in employment; protection and rehabilitation for children who have suffered exploitation or abuse of any kind.

Participation rights

These rights secure children's freedom to express opinions, have a say in matters affecting their own lives, to join associations and to assemble peacefully. As their capacities develop, children should have an increased opportunity to participate in the activities of society, in preparation for adulthood.

The UNCRC (Unicef, 1989) marks a shift from a perspective that predominantly sees children as in need of special protection, still prevalent in the principles of 1959 Declaration of the Rights of the Child to viewing children also as rights holders. The need of the child for special protection is visible in the Preamble of the UNCRC (Unicef, 1989, p3) which states: 'The child, by reason of his physical and mental immaturity needs special safeguards and care, including appropriate legal protection, before as well as after birth'. Such a position, as Woodhead (2015) suggests, entails that children's needs are recognised and responded to by adults. This, he argues, places children in a vulnerable position as it relies on adults' assumptions of what these needs are, and how they can be met. Taking a global perspective, Woodhead (2015) reminds us that children's needs will be viewed differently, depending on the culture and their particular context. It follows this may also apply to any culturally diverse society and community.

Taking a closer look at the notion of aligning with a needs perspective and how it may contrast with a right's perspective, we draw on the work of Jonsson (1998, cited in Koren, 2004, p3). This can be seen in table below and offers a useful resource as a starting point for further reflection (Table 1.1):

Needs perspective	Rights perspective
A child is a passive recipient	A child is an active participant
Needs imply goals – including partial goals	Rights imply that all children (100%) should be served
Needs can be met without sustainability	Rights must be met with sustainability
Needs can be ranked in a hierarchy	Rights cannot be hierarchically organised
Needs do not necessarily involve duties	Rights involve duties
Needs are associated with promises	Rights are associated with obligations
Needs may vary across cultures and settings	Rights are universal
Needs can be met through charity	Charity is not acceptable in a rights approach
Meeting needs often depends on political will	Realising rights depends on political choice

Table 1.1   Needs perspective versus rights perspective

Source: Jonsson (1998), cited in Koren (2004, p3).

Reflective task

- How would you differentiate between a need and a right?

- Can you give examples to some of the above points?

- Consider the policies in your early childhood setting or workplace: Are children's needs or rights more prevalent in these policies? Why might this be and what is the impact on children, families and staff?

As we have seen above, protection rights are a cornerstone of the UNCRC (Unicef, 1989) and ensure children are safeguarded against all forms of abuse, neglect and exploitation. However, another cornerstone is the participation rights most visible in article 12 giving every child the right to express their views and to be listened to in all matters affecting them. Woodhead (2005, p92) highlights 'while an image of the child in need can be linked to protection rights, an image of the competent child is more consistent with participatory rights.' Both these images are visible in the UNCRC (Unicef, 1989) as it views children as human beings who need to be protected as well as affirmed in their right to being listened to and participate in society.

Children's rights, social justice and inclusion

Reflective task

Use your reflective journal or a notepad to write your responses.

(Continued)

(Continued)

- What is your understanding of social justice?

- Consider the term 'social' – write down all that comes to mind when you think of 'social'.

- Now consider the term 'justice'. What comes to mind? – add to your notes

When considering 'social' you may have thought of 'society', 'community' or 'being together' and maybe the term justice led you to terms such as 'fairness' or got you thinking of the 'legal system' within a country.

According to Miller (2005, in Walker, 2011, p47), 'social justice involves a commitment to ensuring each person gets a fair share of the benefits, and carries a fair share of the responsibilities, of living together in a community'. Social justice relates to issues of inclusion and exclusion and, therefore, considers participation rights of the UNCRC (Unicef, 1989). This definition serves as a reminder that responsibilities go hand in hand with rights being held. Article 42 of the UNCRC (Unicef, 1989) highlights the importance of adults working with children to develop their knowledge and understanding of their rights. In the following section, we will look at how practitioners can support children's rights in early childhood settings and aim for social justice. In addition, inclusive practice will be considered by drawing on an example relating to Special Educational Needs and Disabilities (SEND) and it will be demonstrated how legislation and practice interlink. You may find it useful to read Chapter 2 when considering the legislative and policy context discussed in this chapter.

The UNCRC's (Unicef, 1989, p4) article 2 sets out that the rights of the child apply to each child 'without discrimination of any kind, irrespective of the child's or his or her parent's or legal guardian's race, colour, sex, language, religion, political or other opinion, national, ethnic or social origin, property, disability, birth or other status' and that state parties need to 'ensure that the child is protected against all forms of discrimination or punishment on the basis of the status, activities, expressed opinions, or beliefs of the child's parents, legal guardians, or family members.' In the United Kingdom, the UNCRC (Unicef, 1989), as well as Acts of Parliament, such as the Children Act 1989 and the Equality Act 2010 build the legal foundation of the right of the child to inclusion and participation. It is important to note that the UNCRC (Unicef, 1989) has been strengthened by the duty in the Childcare Act 2006, which requires Local Authorities (LAs) in England to listen and include the views of children in the development of Early Childhood Services. To realise these rights in practice, practitioners' responsibilities entail that all children are fully included in EY settings. To this end, it is important for students and practitioners to have knowledge and understanding of issues regarding children's rights and inclusion. The definition by the Early Childhood Forum (ECF) is particularity suitable in this respect: in its value statement the ECF (2022) defines inclusion as a 'process of identifying, understanding, and breaking down the barriers to participation and belonging'.

Reflective task

Inclusion is a process of identifying, understanding and breaking down the barriers to participation and belonging.

(ECF, 2022)

Reflect on this definition of inclusion in the light of your learning on social justice.

- What does this definition mean for the role of the early childhood practitioner?
- What does this mean for children in early childhood settings?
- What is the importance of legislation and relevant policies in making inclusion a lived experience for all children in early childhood settings?

Inclusion and Special Educational Needs (SEN): Legislation

In England, EY practice in relation to SEND is guided by the SEND Code of Practice (Department for Education (DfE) and Department of Health (DoH), 2015). It is the result of changes made to the then SEN Code of Practice (Department for Education and Skills, 2001) due to the Children and Families Act 2014, which came into force in September 2014. The SEND Code of Practice (DfE and DoH, 2015, p13) is statutory, which means it must be adhered to by 'all early years providers in the maintained, private, voluntary and independent sectors' which are funded by the local authority. The term 'special educational need' or 'SEN' as it relates to the EY is defined in the SEND Code of Practice (DfE and DoH, 2015, p15): 'A child or young person has SEN if they have a learning difficulty or disability which calls for special educational provision to be made for him or her'. The Equality Act 2010 includes the Disability Discrimination Act 1995 which defines disability as: 'A physical or mental impairment which has a substantial and long-term adverse effect on a person's ability to perform normal day-to-day activities'.

The Early Years Foundation Stage (EYFS) (DfE, 2021a, p6) in its overarching principles of the 'unique child' and 'learning and development' recognises that children develop and learn at different rates. Within the EYFS (DfE, 2021a) planning must be based on these principles and any adjustments made accordingly. The value of inclusion is implicit in the EYFS (DfE, 2021a, p6) framework as it 'covers the education and care of all children in early years provision, including children with SEND'.

Reflective task

Child M has cerebral palsy* and wears a support bandage on her right hand. During circle time when children are holding hands there have been occasions where a child would refuse to hold Child M's hand. You observe Child M is now reluctant to participate in circle time.

- What would you do?

- What rights need to be considered here and why?

- Would your actions link to any policies and procedures within your setting? If yes, which one's?

*According to the National Health Service (NHS) (2022a) 'cerebral palsy is the name for a group of lifelong conditions that affect movement and co-ordination. It's caused by a problem with the brain that develops before, during or soon after birth'.

As you consider your response, keep in mind children have the right:

- To be protected from abuse (Human Rights Act 1998)

- To have an education as stated in article 28 of the UNCRC (Unicef, 1989)

- Not to be discriminated against because of their race, colour, sex, disability, language and beliefs as outlined in article 2 of the UNCRC (Unicef, 1989), and article 2 of Protocol 1 of the Human Rights Act 1998

- Not to be treated or punished in a way that is cruel or meant to make them feel bad about themselves which is expressed in articles 19 and 37 of the UNCRC (Unicef, 1989)

(Adapted from Jones, 2011)

How to support children's rights in settings

It is crucial when considering the rights of the child within our settings to be mindful that these may clash with those of the child within the home. Jones and Welch (2018) stress that parents' or carers' beliefs and values will shape their expectations of the child and how they relate to the child, which may not be in keeping with either the principles of the UNCRC (Unicef, 1989) or with expectations of government or setting policies.

Several service providers including schools have begun to reflect children's rights in their individual policies. They may call it a 'Children's Rights Policy' and cite the UNCRC (Unicef, 1989) as a source.

Reflective task

Look at the policies within your setting or search for early childhood setting policies published online and identify those that relate to children's rights.

- What are the most common themes and rights that run through them? For example, the right to have your views heard and be listened to may be found in a number of setting policies.

- Are there other rights that are promoted within the setting policies?

- If you cannot find children's rights reflected in the setting policies, what could be done about this? (It may be helpful to look at Chapter 2 on how policies can be developed).

Reggio Emilia in northern Italy is an example of EY practice where children's rights are taken seriously and fundamental to their practice, provision, curriculum and pedagogy and where the rights of children, teachers and parents are embraced. Malaguzzi (1996) highlights practitioners' responsibilities to:

1. Safeguard children's rights

2. Question whether all children are seen as equal

3. Consider whether practitioners are meeting individual needs

4. Explore how the child may be respected

Rinaldi (2021) defines the pedagogy of Reggio Emilia as a pedagogy of listening and emphasises that in Reggio Emilia children are seen as innately social beings able to listen and desiring to be heard. Seen from Rinaldi's (2021, p40) perspective the setting is a space to offer the context for 'multiple listening' where the teacher is supportive of facilitating learning through the shared and collaborative endeavour of children and adults 'listening to others and themselves'.

Respect for the views of the child

Inspired by the pedagogy of Reggio Emilia, Clark and Moss developed the Mosaic approach, where the participatory and active nature of a pedagogy of listening is visible (Clark, 2017). Within the Mosaic approach listening is seen as a process of communication involving 'hearing, interpreting, and constructing meanings not limited to the spoken word' (Clark, 2017, p23). Malaguzzi (in Edwards et al., 2011) presents the multiple ways in which young children express themselves as the 'Hundred Languages', and these can be seen similarly in, for example, the visual representations children create within the Mosaic approach or when children's active participation in matters that affect them is fostered through child conferencing. A commitment to listen to the voice of children is evident in these approaches and clearly realises the UNCRC's (Unicef, 1989) article 12: the child's right to have their opinion heard on matters affecting them. The many ways children can express themselves offer them a voice appropriate to their age and maturity, so due weight can be given to their views. When in 2008 the EYFS (DCSF, 2008) framework became statutory for children from birth to 5 years, it put forward that EY practitioners demonstrate inclusivity of practice through actively participating in equality of opportunity and anti-discriminatory practice for all children. This includes the legal requirement to listen to young children under the Childcare Act 2006, section 3 (5). As discussed above early childhood services have a crucial role to play in developing a listening culture which nurtures day-to-day listening. Ensuring the right to be listened to is a lived experience in early childhood practice and provision, it is important for students and practitioners to regularly reflect on, and if required, take action to enable a listening approach. A commitment to a listening culture for example will be visible in the way day-to-day decisions are made within the setting.

Reflective task

- What do we mean by listening to children?

- Does your setting have a listening culture?

- Can you listen to children through looking at pictures, drawings or their role play?

- How can your observations of children support a listening culture within the setting?

- How can practitioners' values and beliefs impact on implementing a listening approach in the setting?

Advocacy in practice

The verb 'to advocate' means to support someone (in our context it would be children) by means of backing up their actions or a right, the advocate believes they have. For example, in the context of a student, a teacher can advocate for their students to ensure their right to a fair grading system. Similarly, a parent can advocate for their child to receive special support in school if needed, for example, when their child has SEND. An advocate's role is to make sure that children's views, opinions and experiences are considered when decisions are being made that will affect them and their future. This is different from representing the 'best interests' of the child as is sometimes the case when professionals make decisions affecting the child. An example of this would be when decisions are made relating to safeguarding concerns.

A definition of advocacy and the role of the advocate has been put together by the Scottish Government (2014): 'Advocacy is about supporting a child to express their own needs and views and to make informed decisions on matters which influence their lives. Advocates do not make choices for children – instead, they support children and young people to make their own choices'. In practice, an advocate should adjust their support as appropriate to the child's age and maturity. This can influence children's development positively; it helps to improve self-esteem and their ability to build resilience throughout childhood and aids their transition to adulthood and eventual independence.

The Children Act 1989 states that young people must be respected and listened to. As EY practitioners you are advocates for children's rights. Therefore, your role is to put forward a case on behalf of, and together with, children wherever possible. For example, to make each child's case to external professionals such as social workers or speech and language therapists, who are working closely with you. In addition to support children's choices and decisions within their daily life at the setting, provided, of course, that their behaviour or choices do not adversely affect other children. It is important not to forget that parents or carers are also advocates for their own children's rights. Unicef (2010, p3) defines advocacy as going beyond what we do within the setting: 'advocacy is the deliberate process, based on demonstrated evidence, to directly and indirectly influence decision makers, stakeholders and relevant audiences to support and implement actions that contribute to the fulfilment of children's and women's rights.'

Advocacy can be seen as a human right both for the advocate and for the individual whose rights are being protected. Children need advocates as they cannot look after their own interests. Parents are supposed to do this for them however some do not or cannot do this, for example, due to lack of parental capacity. Children are not always heard by the adults who make decisions that affect them most. These include a range of professionals, governments who decide what resources will and will not be available to their families, or to the children themselves by welfare workers, magistrates and by the police.

There can be barriers to putting advocacy into practice. Advocacy often relates to different aspects of children's lives such as care, education, health and welfare and when these are dealt with by different government offices, advocacy can be delayed due to the complexity of these departments working in unison. Children rely on adults to be sincere advocates for them. When professionals perceive children as passive participants, they may not necessarily involve them or listen to their views, and this may impact negatively on children's agency in the decision making process. Boylan and Dalrymple (2011) highlight that for many children and young people the systems in operation can be disempowering, rather than working for their rights, which means, at times, children and young people are not viewed as citizens. For this reason, advocacy must go beyond practical actions, it should actively promote citizenship.

Reflective task

- In what ways do you advocate for children in your setting?

- What may be some of the barriers or limitation for advocacy?

- How may you overcome these?

Summary

This chapter began with an exploration of how children and childhood can be understood with the aim of developing an understanding of the child as rights holder. To be able to gain an understanding of the wider context, and to broaden our perspectives on children's rights, we looked into the history of United Nations Convention on the Rights of the Child (Unicef, 1989) and related treaties across the globe as well as within the context of UK legislation. When considering the impact of these perspectives and children's rights on practice, we highlighted that issues of social justice and inclusion are inseparable from realising children's rights approach in the setting and here we focussed on the role of the practitioner. We put forward the need for and importance of the practitioner to be an advocate for the children in their care. The reflective tasks within this chapter have given you opportunity to reflect on, challenge and develop your perspectives on children, their rights and advocacy.

2   The impact of legislation and policies on provision and practice

Policy has an important impact on the daily life of early years practitioners, whatever their role or setting.

(Fitzgerald and Kay, 2016, pix)

Why is knowledge and understanding of legislation and policy important for practitioners and how may this impact on their practice?

Early Years (EY) practitioners sometimes see legislation and policies as something that does not directly affect them, the work they do or what they provide. However, it is important that practitioners embrace policies in a positive way and realise their role and importance within EY practice.

This chapter aims to support practitioners in becoming more comfortable with the policies they are working with in their setting. We hope it will enable practitioners to develop, shape and influence policy in future.

CHAPTER OVERVIEW

In this chapter we aim to help you develop your understanding of:

- The historical and political context of legislation and policies in the context of early childhood provision in the United Kingdom

- Relevant legislation and policy relating to the context of early childhood practice

- What policies are and how they are developed

- The impact of policies on settings and lives of practitioners, children and families

---

You will find that Chapters 1, 3, 4, 5, 7 and 8 link closely to the topics discussed within this chapter.

This chapter links to the relevant criteria for:

Early Years Educator (Department for Education and National College for Teaching and Leadership, 2019)

- 1.10 Promote equality of opportunity and anti-discriminatory practice;

- 5.1 Know the legal requirements and guidance on health and safety, security, confidentiality of information, safeguarding and promoting the welfare of children;

- 5.7 Carry out risk assessment and risk management in line with policies and procedures;

- 5.8 Understand safeguarding policies and procedures, including child protection, recognise when a child is in danger or at risk of abuse and know how to act to protect them.

Early Childhood Graduate Practitioner Competencies (Early Childhood Studies Degree Network, 2019).

- 3.2 Demonstrate the application of knowledge about health, well-being and safety to practice, including the importance of policies and legislation;

- 3.3 Apply data protection legislation to practice;

- 5.1 Know the wider legislative and statutory guidance for safeguarding including child protection, whistle blowing, digital safety and how these are articulated into setting policy;

- 9.1 Demonstrate self-awareness and knowledge of anti-discriminatory practice, promoting social justice and the importance of valuing difference, including gender, ethnicity, religious affiliation and sexual orientation.

Historical and political perspectives of UK legislation and policies and the impact of these on EY provision

In order to understand the legislation that guide early childhood practice, it is important to be clear about the political and historical context surrounding these pieces of legislation while acknowledging how they shape policies and procedures. Prior to the late 1990s, there had not been a great deal of discussion and focus on EY policies as it was not the main priority for the then Conservative government. However, when Tony Blair came to power in 1997, one of his key priorities and eventual policy was geared towards EY. The focus was on improving outcomes and the life chances for all children, particularly those who were considered as being the most disadvantaged in society and who often lived in deprived areas and communities. The development of Sure Start Local Programmes and then Children Centres were introduced to help bolster and support this policy.

The introduction of the Ten-Year Childcare Strategy published in 2004 (HM Treasury et al., 2004) set out the Labour government's policy programme for childcare and early education. It clarified the Government's vision which was to ensure that every child gets the best start in life and to give parents more choice and support them in being able to balance work and family life. The strategy saw the planned increase of the quantity, availability and accessibility of suitable, flexible childcare particularly for working mothers and also free nursery education for all 4- and later also 3-year-olds (Labour Party, 1997). This policy has been developed further aiming to support 2-year-olds attending settings. However, it is not universal for all 2-year-olds but for the most disadvantaged as there is a strict criteria in being able to access this funding, as you will see below.

The plan to reduce and eliminate child poverty was supported by the introduction of the Child Poverty Act 2010. The purpose of the Child Poverty Act 2010 was the 'eradication of child poverty' and to create a framework to monitor progress at a national and local level. It set out in legislation a requirement to meet four child poverty targets by 2020. This required governments to publish a clear strategy every three years of how they are meeting these targets and report annually on progress. The Act also placed duties on devolved administrations, and on local authorities in England.

Free education and childcare for 2-year-olds

According to GOV.UK (2022a) 2-year-olds can get free childcare if they live in England and get one of the following benefits:

- Income Support

- income-based Jobseeker's Allowance (JSA)

- income-related Employment and Support Allowance (ESA)

- Universal Credit, and your household income is £15,400 a year or less after tax, not including benefit payments

- child tax credits, and your household income is £16,190 a year or less before tax

- the guaranteed element of Pension Credit

- the Working Tax Credit 4-week run on (the payment you get when you stop qualifying for Working Tax Credit)

2-year-olds can also get free childcare if they:

- are looked after by a local authority

- have a statement of special education needs (SEN) or an education, health and care (EHC) plan

- get Disability Living Allowance

- have left care under an adoption order, special guardianship order or a child arrangements order

What are policies?

Fitzgerald and Kay (2016) define policies as stated intentions, or formal statements of a course of action, that guide practice and procedure. Policies within settings will set out how they intend to address and enact government legislation or guidance, for example, equality policies and the Special Educational Needs Code of Practice (DfE and DoH, 2015) guidance.

Moss (2003) expresses how policies reflect the views of government at the time and are heavily influenced by the dominant culture and socio-economic context of the area or country. You may have noticed from practice that some policies are setting-specific, for example, linked to wearing a specific work uniform. However, most policies are informed by legislation, or are required by Ofsted, for example, safeguarding, health and safety and employment vetting policies (Ofsted, 2019a).

It is important that practitioners embrace policies in a positive way and realise that these are important within EY for several reasons. They provide guidelines and procedures on how various situations should be handled in order to minimise risk within settings as well as enabling effective practice and provision (Miller and Hevey, 2012). EY settings use a wide range of policies to inform and support practice and provision.

Reflective task

Look at the range of policies being implemented within your own setting:

- What areas of practice are the focus of these policies within your setting?

- Why do you think these policies are important?

Policies often come with guidance. For example, in relation to safeguarding we have the 'Working Together to Safeguard Children' document (HM Government, 2018a). Training and guidance is often offered to help support practitioners and other professionals' knowledge and understanding of what needs to be done particularly 'if you're worried that a child is being abused' (DfE, 2015).

Although practitioners may feel some policies may be a waste of time, difficult to follow, understand or just annoying and without purpose it is important they realise and appreciate that there are reasons why these policies are in place. Understanding the context for the policies will help you to understand the reasons for them and realise why they need to be implemented fully (Miller and Hevey, 2012). Simpson and Connor (2011, cited in Miller and Hevey, 2012, p2) describe this as 'policy literacy' which 'aims to make recipients and practitioners of social welfare more critical and discriminating readers, performers and producers of policies'. They describe three phases in the achievement of policy literacy:

1. Understanding policies and their impacts on the lives of children and families

2. Learning to analyse and question the basis, construction and coverage of policies, including what may have been missed out

3. Exploring underlying issues and principles behind policy formation, including: whose interests a particular policy ultimately serves? Whose viewpoints are represented (or ignored)? What alternatives are available?

How do policies and legislation work together?

Legislation are laws that have been passed by our UK Parliament and from the date when implemented become statutory. For example, you may be familiar with the Children Act 1989, Children Act 2004, Childcare Act 2006 and the Equality Act 2010 (these are commonly referred to within EY and will be discussed in more detail within this chapter). Many of the policies and procedures that you follow within EY (Equality Policy, Inclusion Policy, Safeguarding Policy, Curriculum Policy) have been written and implemented due to particular pieces of legislation. Legislation and its resulting policies and procedures are intended to guarantee the welfare and safety of all individuals. It is important that they are followed to prevent any negative impact on anyone's life (Fitzgerald and Kay, 2016).

Reflective task

- What are the different types of policies that you have or are aware of within your setting?

- Do they link to any pieces of legislation? If yes which ones?

- How do they impact on the setting, children and families?

- What frustrates you or is challenging with implementing the policies? What changes would you make if you could and why?

- How would your setting function without any policies or procedures? What may be the consequences?

How policies may be developed in a variety of settings?

Policies are generally written documents with clear statements. There is usually a clear aim and rationale for the policy. As discussed earlier, the development of policies will have been influenced as a result of government legislation (nationally) or as a result of an incident or issue that may have arisen within the setting or community (locally).

It must be clear who the policy applies to, for example, your work with children, parents or other stakeholders. The policy should make it clear what is acceptable behaviour or what you should be doing, which is usually referred to as procedures. An example of a procedure would be carrying out a risk assessment before taking children out on visits. It is important that policies are reviewed regularly to see if they are effective and still fit for purpose. There is usually a named person who will take the lead to write, monitor and be responsible for policy implementation. However, there may be sub-groups or committees that come together to support the lead person with this. All policies must be dated and updated when reviewed to ensure everyone is clear which copy is current and being used.

There will have been a variety of tasks to be completed before getting to the implementation stage of any policy. For example, it will need to be established whether there is a legal responsibility for having the policy, as is the case, for example, with safeguarding. Many checks would have been gone through to ensure the policy is clear and accurate. It is important to consult with the relevant stakeholders (children where possible and if relevant, parents, staff, management committee members or governing body) and service users with the aim to get their views or perspectives on how it may affect or impact them whether directly or indirectly. The policy will have to be approved, and this is usually the responsibility of the man-agement committee, or relevant governing body. They will ultimately sign off and be responsible for the policy and, therefore, clarity needs to be applied to the following:

- Is the policy clear or does it need additional guidance?

- How will the policy be implemented and by whom?

- When will the policy come into effect and how will this be communicated to the staff, parents or other relevant stakeholders?

- Will training be required to support the implementation of the policy?

- What kind of monitoring and reporting processes need to be put in place?

- When the policy will be reviewed and revised?

Reflective task

Consider the below case study.

(Continued)

(Continued)

Case study

Roland is three years old. He lives with his mum and dad and three older siblings, very close to the nursery. He is a bright and cheerful boy although he is slightly late developing his language skills. He will sometimes become frustrated when people do not understand him.

Like most children, Roland occasionally has bruises on his arms and legs. He is very active and particularly enjoys playing in his garden at home and riding the bikes at high speed in the playground.

One day at 3pm, you find Roland silently weeping in the toilet area. At first, he will not say why he is upset, but after some gentle coaxing, he tells you he is frightened to go home because he 'has made daddy angry and will be punished'. Later that day Roland is collected by his 18-year-old brother, which is not unusual. He refuses to leave the nursery and is screaming and shouting. His brother admits that their father can be violent when he is annoyed.

- What are your concerns about Roland?

- What are your first actions as a practitioner?

- Are there any policies and procedures to help guide you on what to do? If yes which one?

- If you are not aware (or new to the setting) of any policies or procedures, what would you do?

- What may be the impact of relevant policies and procedures on practitioners, children and families?

It is important to be clear about the known facts while acknowledging any gaps in your knowledge and understanding without making assumptions or being judgemental. You may have questions about some of the points; note down what these may be and discuss these with a colleague, tutor or your mentor.

What is the impact of legislation on setting policy and the lives of practitioners, children and families?

For many that have been working within the EY for a number of years it would be impossible to not have noticed the many changes following the introduction of a range of legislations and policies. We will consider a few of these in Table 2.1.

Legislation	Impact/benefits on the setting	Impact/benefits on children	Impact/benefits on parents/families
Children Act 1989	The child's needs are highlighted as being 'Paramount' and must be prioritised. Local Authorities (LAs) and professionals are to work in partnership with each other.	The child's voice must be heard and considered (where possible) when decisions are being made about their life. Children's cultural and religious needs are to be considered when important decisions are being made about their lives.	Professionals have a duty to work with parents who have Parental Responsibility also known as PR in order to achieve the best outcome for their children.
Children Act 2004	It is important that settings focus on the well-being of children. Particularly around the areas of child protection. Following the death of children such as Victoria Climbie multi-professional working is seen as key in improving effective local working to safeguard and promote children's well-being.	The previous 'Every Child Matters' agenda has been incorporated within policy and aims to: 1. Ensure children are healthy 2. Keep children safe 3. Help them to enjoy themselves and achieve 4. Ensure they make a positive contribution 5. The hope is that long term they are able to achieve economic well-being	The Common Assessment Framework (CAF) or Early Help Assessment can enable parents/families to get additional support for their children and often for themselves, e.g., free nursery place, attendance on a parenting programme.
Childcare Act 2006	A responsibility to support better outcomes for children aged 0–5. The introduction of the Early Years Foundation Stage (EYFS) within all settings (DCSF, 2008). Settings are required to follow this framework for learning, development and care for children from birth to 5.	The EYFS makes it clear that each child is unique and therefore each child will be encouraged to develop at their own pace and that their individual needs will be met. This will help them as they are being prepared and ready for school at 5 years.	Parents/families can be confident that there is a standard of EY provision (set through the framework) at all settings. Allowing their children opportunities to develop important skills and knowledge. Settings are required to work in partnership with parents ensuring that they are being consulted about and involved in their children's learning and development. This will also support continuity and learning at home.
Equality Act 2010	All settings are to have an equality policy/statement. Staff are to be treated equally and where necessary 'minor adjustments' to be made to support them at work.	All children are to be treated equally and individual needs are to be met.	Parents/families to also be treated fairly and their needs are to also be considered, e.g., if they have a disability.

(Continued)

Table 2.1   (Continued)

Legislation	Impact/benefits on the setting	Impact/benefits on children	Impact/benefits on parents/families
Children and Families Act 2014	Settings are required to ensure that there are specific arrangements in place to support children's Special Educational Needs and Disability.	Children who get additional support are more able to succeed in future and therefore achieve better outcomes and life chances.	Additional resources are to be made available to support their children.

Table 2.1   Legislation and their impacts

The Equality Act 2010

All settings that follow the EYFS (DfE, 2021a) will have their own equality policy following government legislation. The Equality Act 2010 is in place to protect everyone against discrimination and to promote equality. The Equality Act 2010 highlights certain characteristics which are protected from discrimination under the law. These include age; disability; religion or belief; race; gender reassignment; sex and sexual orientation.

The Act also aligns with the UNCRC (Unicef, 1989) where children's rights apply to all children without discrimination for example in the areas of identity, race, religion or sex. They also have the right to freedom of religion or belief, and the right to an education. This has been discussed in depth in Chapter 1: Perspectives on Children's Rights.

The Children Act 1989

The Children Act 1989 was one of the first pieces of legislation introduced for the safety and well-being of children, focussing on the child's well-being up to the age of 18. The Act affords every child the right to protection from violence and neglect, as well as the right to have investigations made to safeguard their health and well-being. There are general principles set out in Section 1 of the Children Act 1989. It states the child's well-being is *'paramount'*. The Act introduced the notion of *'significant harm'* as the threshold which validates compulsory intervention in family life in children's best interests. Section 47 of the Act states that harm or the risk of harm is due to the lack of sufficient parental care or control.

The Act also highlights and introduces the terminology 'Parental Responsibility' (PR). As practitioners it is important that you are aware which adult has PR (it may not always be the parents). Those with PR can make or be involved in the important decisions necessary in a child's life including issues relating to where a child should live, education (for example, where a child should go to school and the right to receive school reports), health and medical treatment (for example, whether a child should receive medical treatment or vaccinations). This also includes 'changing a child's name, religion (for example, what religion, if any, a child should follow or receive instruction in) and, going abroad, either permanently or on holiday (you may be committing an offence if you do not seek consent from everyone with PR before taking a child abroad)' (Rights of Woman, 2014, p1).

The Children Act 2004

This Act builds on the Children Act 1989 and makes it clear that everyone including organisations that work with children have a responsibility in helping to safeguard them and promote their welfare. The Children Act 2004 gives guidance to anyone working within an educational or non-educational setting of how children should be looked after by law. The principles of the Act follow what many of you are familiar with as the Every Child Matters agenda (The Stationary Office, 2003) which is no longer current policy. See below what the five outcomes were:

1. Allow children to be healthy

2. Help children to be happy and enjoy life

3. Allow children to remain safe in their environments

4. Help achieve economic stability for the future of children

5. Help make a positive contribution to children's lives

The Childcare Act 2006

The Childcare Act 2006 continues to be an important piece of legislation. It places specific duties on local authorities, particularly to improve the outcomes for all young children. The Act has reformed and simplified EY regulation and inspection arrangements, providing a new integrated education and care quality framework for pre-school children and for the then introduced Ofsted Childcare Register.

The Early Years Foundation Stage (EYFS) was established under the Childcare Act 2006 and is a framework for learning, development and care for children. It describes what is considered as high-quality EY provision in England attended by children from birth up to the age of 5 years. Within your setting, there may be policies that you follow which are linked to this piece of legislation, for example, an EY curriculum or planning policy. The Act also requires the local authority to work in partnership with the private, voluntary and independent sector to secure sufficient childcare (types of provision, opening times, age range, registration status) for all parents who choose to work or are in training and in preparation for work.

All local authorities have a duty to provide information (education, health, leisure and parenting), advice and assistance on childcare and other services (type of service, who to contact, opening times, cost). Families and service users will be signposted to information, this may include relevant websites and written materials. It is the local authority's responsibility to help sign post parents to the most suitable provision.

Reflective task

- Refer to a copy of the Childcare Act 2006 (summary)

- Read and list the different ways that you believe the Childcare Act 2006 impacts on children's lives and early education (What maybe some of the issues?)

What did you learn from completing this task? How may it support your work with children and families?

The Children and Families Act 2014

This Act came into force in order to support parents and carers of children and young people aged 0–25 years who have SEN or disabilities. The Act became law on 13 March 2014. This summary refers to the parts of the Act relating to people with SEN or disabilities and their families. There are four key principles in the Act that local authorities must follow.

1. They must consider the views, wishes and feelings of the child, young person and their parents (also linked to the Children Act 1989)

2. Involve the child, young person and their parents in decisions that affect them (also linked to the UNCRC (Unicef, 1989) and the Children Act 1989)

3. Give the child, young person and their parents the information and support they need to be involved in decision making (also linked to the UNCRC (Unicef, 1989))

4. Support the child, young person and their parents to achieve the best possible outcomes (also linked to the Childcare Act 2006)

Summary

This chapter has given you knowledge and understanding of the importance of legislation, policies and how they have come about and why they are so important to practice. The table within the chapter demonstrates the ways in which policies can impact on the lives of practitioners, children, parents and families. The case studies and tasks aimed to help you to reflect on your practice and consider areas for development and additional information.

Although settings can have excellent policies that are clearly written, they are no use if staff are unaware of these or do not follow them. Policies and procedures need to be useful and supportive to staff in order to be effectively implemented and not put on a shelf somewhere gathering dust (Fitzgerald and Kay, 2016).

3 Working with diverse families and a range of professionals

The family is the basic institution through which children learn who they are, where they fit into society and what kind of futures they are likely to experience.

(Clark, 1983, pix)

Why is knowledge and understanding of working with diverse families and a range of professionals important for practitioners and how may this impact on their practice?

Partnership working with families or carers and a range of professionals is firmly embedded today in early childhood practice, supported by the Early Years Foundation Stage (EYFS) Framework (Department for Education (DfE), 2021a) and the wider legislative framework of the United Kingdom. Practitioners, who continue to develop their skills and knowledge on this aspect of their role, make successful partnership working a reality for all stakeholders. This chapter will explore working with diverse families and professionals from a range of perspectives and what this may look like in practice. It will explore the importance of working with diverse families and a range of professionals who work within the Early Years (EY) and will consider what some of the challenges may be when working in partnership with families and professionals.

CHAPTER OVERVIEW

In this chapter we aim to help you develop your understanding of:

- The historical perspectives on working with families and professionals
- Concepts of family and the socio-cultural contexts of parenting
- Perspectives of the child in the context of the family
- The crucial role of the parents or carers in the child's development and learning within a diverse society

(Continued)

CHAPTER OVERVIEW continued

- The professional skills needed in working in partnership with families, carers and in multi-professional teams

- A range of approaches to assessing young children and their families in a multi-professional context

You will find that Chapters 2, 4, 7 and 8 link closely to the topics discussed within this chapter.

This chapter links to the relevant criteria for:

Early Years Educator (Department for Education and National College for Teaching and Leadership, 2019)

- 1.5 Understand the importance of promoting diversity, equality and inclusion, fully reflecting cultural differences and family circumstances;

- 2.2 Ensure plans fully reflect the stage of development, individual needs and circumstances of children;

- 2.11 Plan and provide activities to meet additional needs, working in partnership with parents and/or carers and other professionals, where appropriate;

- 3.5 Discuss children's progress and plan the next stages in their learning with the key person, colleagues, parents and/or carers;

- 6.2 Work in partnership with parents and/or carers to help them recognise and value the significant contributions they make to the child's health, well-being, learning and development;

- 6.3 Encourage parents and/or carers to take an active role in the child's play, learning and development.

Early Childhood Graduate Practitioner Competencies (Early Childhood Studies Degree Network, 2019)

- 7.1 Evidence understanding of the importance of partnership with parents and/or caregivers in their role as infants and young children's first educators;

- 7.2 Demonstrate in practice the co-construction of learning in respectful partnership with parents and/or caregivers;

(Continued)

(Continued)

- 7.3 Apply knowledge to practice, about the diversity of family life and society;

- 7.4 Demonstrate skills in communicating and working in partnership with families.

Historical perspectives on working with families

In order to understand today's practice of working with families, we begin by shedding light on how working with families has evolved in England. The introduction of compulsory schooling with the Education Act 1880 was a significant factor in changing how children and childhood were understood towards the end of the 19th century. Its social and cultural impact could be seen as separating a child's lived experiences from those of the adult. The concurrent abolition of child labour paved the way to a perception of children away from having economic value towards having emotional value as identified by Zelizer (1985, in Hendrick, 2012) and you may look back at the introduction chapter for more contextual information.

Seeing the child as part of their family when they are educated outside the home emerged when Froebel's (1782–1853) ideas begun to have an impact in England with the establishment of the Froebel Society in London in 1874. The purpose of Froebel's kindergarten was to add to and extend children's learning at home rather than replace it (Gillard, 2006). Later pioneers such as Grace Owen proposed for nursery schools to 'achieve a real unity with the home-life', also embraced in the Hadow Report (1933, p103, in Gillard, 2006). This report paved the way for the expansion of nursery provision and development of working practices with families based on co-operation. In its conclusion, the report recognises the positive impact of co-operation between parents and school on health promoting the idea of the school as having a social function (Gillard, 2006).

The consensus at the time of the Hadow Report 1933 was that children under the age of 2 belong at home, and those over the age of 5 must attend compulsory schooling, and that children between these ages may be spending some time away from home in a nursery school. Recognising that children attending nursery will spend a significant amount of time at home led to the report calling for the curriculum in nursery schools to be adapted into the home learning environment. This was with the expectation of parents actively participating, for example, on issues such as health and hygiene (Fitzgerald, 2010). This perspective, however, resembles a deficit model of working with parents, as it sees parents as agents to the teacher and not as equals (Edwards and Warin, 1999, in Fitzgerald, 2010).

In contrast to the above-mentioned deficit model, McMillan (1860–1931) proposed that her teachers should be part of and have an understanding of the local community in which they work (Jarvis and Liebovich, 2015). Her perspective influenced and shaped the approach to working with parents by promoting nursery education as a 'part of [*children's*] home life' (McMillan, 1919, p29). It was important to McMillan that space and opportunity for children to be active outside should be close to their homes. Her child-centred approach supported the health and well-being of the children in her care and underpinned her positive working practice with parents. This is still visible in models of partnership working with parents today.

The Plowden Report (1967, p37, in Gillard, 2004), although largely focussing on compulsory schooling, strongly promotes participation of parents in schools through a 'close partnership' between schools and parents arguing it will lead to better educational performance. It strengthened and promoted child-centred practice and teaching in schools, and this sentiment is endorsed in its recommendation for under-fives' nursery provision. The report strongly believes that co-operation between nursery and home will only succeed if parents are seen as equal partners in this relationship (Gillard, 2004). The report strongly recommended the expansion of nurseries; however, the gap in provision was largely met by voluntary groups such as the Pre-School Playgroups Association. Here mothers (predominantly at the time) were actively involved in the running of the playgroups which resulted in close parent partnership working.

In May 1998, the then Labour government launched the National Childcare Strategy with the aim to provide affordable, quality childcare in support of children's learning and development by offering every 4-year-old a part-time nursery place, thus enabling parents to carry out relevant training or to work (Nursery World, 2001). This was supported by the Sure Start local programmes launched in 1999 by the Labour government bringing together health services and parenting and family support. At the same time, the introduction of the Curriculum Guidance for the Foundation Stage embedded 'early years practitioners working in partnership with parents and other adults' into early childhood practice (Qualifications and Curriculum Authority, 2000, p6). This approach was strengthened by research such as Melhuish et al. (2001) which demonstrated the importance and impact of the home learning environment (HLE) on children's development. In 2008, we saw the introduction of the Statutory Framework for the EYFS (DCSF, 2008) and its learning and development requirements, with parent partnership remaining at the heart of EY practice throughout the many changes to the framework that followed.

Historical perspectives on working with professionals

As well as a historical perspective when working with parents there is also a historical context to consider when working with other professionals. The focus here is to support your understanding of the importance of working as part of a wider multi-professional team. The Children Act 1989 makes it clear that the welfare of the child is 'paramount' and that it is important to work in partnership with parents and others particularly where they have 'parental responsibility'. The Act highlights the importance of working with other professionals such as social workers to help prevent harm and keep children safe within a parent–partnership approach.

We are all expected to understand and recognise the contribution and responsibilities of a range of professionals who support the work carried out with children and families. This could include a range of professionals such as the Special Educational Needs Coordinator (SENCO), Speech and Language Therapist (SLT), Health Visitor (HV), Social Worker (SW), General Practitioner (GP) and the Police (HM Government, 2018a). Often, as practitioners you may be involved with these professionals when planning for children's individual needs.

You may ask yourself what is integrated or multi-professional working? The now disbanded Children's Workforce Development Council (CWDC, 2008b, p2) highlighted that multi-professional or 'integrated working is when everyone supporting children and young people works together effectively to put the child at the centre, meet their needs and improve their lives'. They also clarify that 'multi-agency working enables different services to join forces in order to prevent problems occurring in the first place. It is an effective way of supporting children, young people and families with additional needs and helping to secure improved outcomes. There are a number of different models of multi-agency working, including fully integrated services, multi-agency teams, multi-agency panels, Teams Around the Child (TAC)' (CWDC, 2008b, p5).

There is a duty on local authorities (LAs) to safeguard and promote the welfare of children in need and those in need of protection (Section 17 and Section 47 of the Children Act 1989). Multi-professional working became a statutory requirement through the Children Act 2004 for all those who work (in a professional capacity) with children and families. If agencies or professionals are approached by colleagues for their help or to get support for their work with children and families, this must be responded to positively. However, these requests need to be in keeping with the professional role and responsibilities of those involved. In addition, the Children Act 2004 requires professionals and agencies to actively make arrangements to promote co-operation between each other.

One of the main purposes of Sure Start Children centres is to work in partnership across professional and agency boundaries, as stipulated by the Childcare Act 2006. This includes working with social workers, health visitors delivering the Healthy Child programme, engagement with midwives and GPs ensuring that vulnerable families are supported into appropriate interventions to improve outcomes for young children.

Concepts of family and the socio-cultural contexts of parenting

What is a family? Considering family in the context of parenting, Dermot and Fowler's (2021, p1) definition of family as an 'institution in which adults are raising children' offers a broad perspective that encompasses the diverse families which practitioners in EY settings are working with. The notion of family itself is socially constructed, which refers to the concept of family being understood and valued as a product of society. In this sense, Hendrick (2012, p9) refers to family as an institution which is 'socially produced, [. . .] rather than naturally or divinely given'. This reflects a subjective understanding of the concept of family, which acknowledges and values each family as unique. This view underpins the values and perspectives endorsed in this chapter. Bronfenbrenner's (1979) ecological systems theory focusses on the external influences on a child's development. This is often presented as an image of the child in the centre, surrounded by the child's immediate environment such as parents or carers and settings and which Bronfenbrenner (1979) refers to as microsystem. The wider influences are the mesosystem, exosystem and macrosystem. This theory aligns with a child-centred approach to practice, informed by an understanding of the family, the wider community and social and cultural factors impacting on a child's development and therefore represents every family as being unique.

Reflective task

Research further on Bronfenbrenner's (1979) ecological systems theory.

- What is your understanding of Bronfenbrenner's ecological systems theory?

- Consider and note down how this theory could support you in working more effectively with children and their families.

Understanding the crucial role of the parents or carers in the child's development and learning within a diverse society

To understand the diversities within society and the role that parents play in their children's learning and development, it is important to consider the makeup of the families who attend your setting and their diverse and unique needs. Defining what constitutes a family is often complex and difficult, as family structures are very different from how they have been in the past say 30, 40 or 50 years. Who is considered or becomes part of a family is very much linked to the context of people's individual lives and how they live it. What appears to be evident is that families generally have a shared history and are more complex in their make-up, which is varied and diverse (Draper and Duffy, 2006). What we do know is that there are different types of families, and below we have highlighted a few examples of the types of families we may be more familiar with:

- **The lone parent family** is clear in the title. These are families led by one parent households.

- **The nuclear family** was more popular in the past and generally consists of two parents and their child or children.

- **Extended families** go beyond what the nuclear family consists of and may include grandparents, aunts, uncles, and cousins all living within the same household.

- **Blended families** is a relatively new name to describe a couple who may have one or more children together or children from a previous relationship who join together and become one family.

- **Foster families** include one or more children living with and being cared for in a family for several reasons, for example, safeguarding concerns, death of one or both parents, parent(s) detained in prison, or ill parent(s).

Whatever the type of families that attend your setting, it is important to respect and try to understand their unique family context in order to work more effectively with them and to support their children. Parents are considered the first and most enduring educators of their children (Early Education, 2021). With this viewpoint, it is clear that if we want better outcomes for children, then you must look to and respect the role of parents and seek the best ways to work in partnership with them.

Reflective task

Consider the different types of families that attend your setting.

Make a list of the varied or different types of families that you work in partnership with. Think about their class, gender, race and ethnicity, sexual orientation, disability and economic circumstances as well as variations in family make-up such as lone parents or blended families.

- How do you or could you provide an environment that makes every family feel welcome and included in the setting?

- How do you or could you involve them in their children's learning and development more effectively?

- What may be some of the challenges or barriers when trying to include families in their children's learning and development?

- How may some of these challenges or barriers be overcome?

Research carried out by the Effective Provision of Pre-School Education (EPPE) study (Sylva et al., 2004) highlights the important role of the parent in supporting children's learning. You may ask what is EPPE? EPPE was the first major European longitudinal study of a national sample of young children's development between the ages of three and seven years. It investigated the effects of pre-school education on approximately 3,000 children. The study also looked at and included information surrounding the background characteristics related to parents, the child's home learning environment and the pre-school settings the children attended. These included a variety of settings such as local authority day nurseries, integrated centres, playgroups, private day nurseries, nursery schools, nursery classes and a number of what they refer to as 'home' children who had no or limited pre-school experience.

There were several key findings from the report (Sylva et al., 2004); however, we have only chosen a couple to highlight which includes discussions of the crucial role or impact parents/families can have on their children's development and learning:

- For all children, the quality of the home learning environment is more important for intellectual and social development than parental occupation, education or income, which has been expressed as: *what parents do is more important than who parents are*.

- Disadvantaged children benefit *significantly* from good quality pre-school experiences, especially where they are with children from different social backgrounds.

If you are not familiar with this research, we urge you to go and look at it in full and consider all the findings. This is a piece of research that all students, practitioners and professionals should be aware of, as it informs the way we work with children, parents and families today.

Working in partnership with parents is seen as key to improving outcomes for all children. Therefore, many settings particularly schools have developed 'Parent Partnership Policies'. These aim to:

- Acknowledge that parents have certain insights in relation to their children's preferences, interests' strengths, skills and challenges

- Ensure effective ongoing communication between the setting and parents

- Letting parents know how their children are progressing

There are different approaches to working with parents and we have found Mac Naughton et al.'s (2003) model helpful. They highlight the following approaches: Firstly, the 'Conforming approach' where the setting is seen as the knowledgeable party and teaches parents and others what is perceived as the *right way* to care for and educate their children. An example of this could be where a workshop or meeting is held informing parents on the most effective way they could help their children learn to read. The 'Reforming approach' involves parents and others in the care and education of their children; however, this is on the setting's terms. These could be arranging meetings where practitioners and parents exchange information about the child so the setting can develop their planning to better meet the child's individual needs. This is seen as benefiting a parent's knowledge and understanding of how their child is progressing, learning and developing at the setting. The final approach is known as the 'Transforming approach', where the setting works together with children, parents and other professionals to improve relationships. This approach creates a closer involvement of parents. Parents and others are invited to work with practitioners to write policies, manage resources and evaluate provision. Often with this approach decisions about what and how children learn are entrusted to parents. This creates a more equitable approach to working with parents and is seen as a strong working partnership.

Reflective task

Mac Naughton et al. (2003) discuss the Conforming, Reforming and Transforming approach to working with parents. Which approach would you say your setting takes or is working towards?

- In what ways do you work effectively with parents? Is this way of working consistent throughout the setting?

- In what ways could you work more effectively with parents?

- Does your setting have a 'Parent Partnership Policy'? If not, why not?

- If you were involved in developing a new 'Parent Partnership Policy', what would it include and why? Who would you include to support you in developing such a policy?

Parental responsibility according to the Children Act 1989 and how this links to the Early Years Foundation Stage (EYFS)

As discussed in Chapter 2 the Children Act 1989 discusses and makes clear what parental responsibility is and who has it (Table 3.1).

Parental responsibility (Children Act 1989)
• Where a child's father and mother were married to each other at the time of his birth, they shall each have parental responsibility for the child.
• [**F2**(1A) Where a child—
• (a) has a parent by virtue of section 42 of the Human Fertilisation and Embryology Act 2008; or
• (b) has a parent by virtue of section 43 of that Act and is a person to whom section 1(3) of the Family Law Reform Act 1987 applies,
• the child's mother and the other parent shall each have parental responsibility for the child.]
• (2) Where a child's father and mother <u>were not married</u> to each other at the time of his birth—
• (a) the mother shall have parental responsibility for the child;
• (b) the father [**F3** shall have parental responsibility for the child if he has acquired it (and has not ceased to have it)] in accordance with the provisions of this Act.

Table 3.1   Parental responsibility according to the Children Act 1989

The EYFS (DfE, 2021a) highlights the importance of settings having accurate information about the child, for example, their full name, date of birth, name and address of every parent and/or carer who is known to the setting. This will include information about any other person who has parental responsibility for the child, which parent(s) the child normally lives with and emergency contact details for parents and/or carers.

Further, the EYFS (DfE, 2021a) is clear and expects partnership working between practitioners with parents or carers where any additional needs maybe identified for the child. This would include support and guidance be given by the setting. In order for this successful partnerships to be established all EY settings need to identify a named key person who will liaise and work closely with the child's parents or carers to ensure the child's care and learning needs are being met both in the setting as well as at home. How the key person approach is embedded in practice may differ from setting to setting. Elfer et al. (2012, p23) define the key person approach as 'an involvement, and individual and recip-rocal commitment between a member of staff and a family' and we will consider what this may look like in early childhood practice in the following section.

Models of partnership with parents

As a relational concept (Papatheodorou, 2009), the keyperson approach puts the needs of the child at the heart of practice, and it is inextricably linked with the parent–partnership approach advocated in the EYFS (DfE, 2021a). It encompasses the family's time throughout the period they attend the setting, often starting with the keyperson supporting the transition from home to the setting, and the keyperson relationship changing when the child moves to a new setting or school.

The key person approach is integral to all aspects of early childhood practice and where the approach is effective you will find the keyperson building trusting relationships with their key children and the family. For example, relationship building may begin with a visit to the home before the child start attending the setting. Good communication with the parents and carers and other professionals involved in the child's care and education is pivotal to the success of this rela-tionship. Keypersons maintain and update records for their key children, and plan for their key children's interests and needs.

Professional skills needed while working in partnership with families, carers and within multi-professional teams

For students and those wanting to develop their skills working with children, families, carers and a range of multi-professionals, it is vital to gain experiences within EY settings. Students are often assigned a mentor to support them in developing core skills. While working alongside the mentor, they may be sharing observations of children, being supported in evaluating these as well as planning for the child's individual needs. Working alongside a mentor observing how they interact with parents will help students see the different ways effective partnerships can work and develop. You will be able to also see some of the challenges or barriers of working in partnership with parents. For example:

- When a parent makes a complaint

- What to do if you suspect that a child may be being abused (DfE, 2015; HM Government, 2018a)

- If a child has a speech and language delay or if there are any other develop-mental concerns

Working with other professionals, for example, being able to observe a session run by a speech and language therapist will help develop your knowledge and understanding of their role and how you can enhance your support to children who may have special education needs or a disability.

What are the core skills and values needed when working with families and other professionals?

Core skills, attributes and knowledge are seen as the basic competences and values needed by professionals when working with children, young people and families. The expectation is that these core skills and values enable 'practitioners to promote equality, respect diversity and challenge stereotypes. It helps to improve life chances for all children and young people, including those who have disabilities and those who are most vulnerable. It promotes partnership working at local level' (DfE, 2010, p5).

There have been debates with regard to relevant core skills needed when working with children, families and other professionals. These were referred to as the common core of skills and knowledge for the children's workforce originally pub-lished by the Children's Workforce Development Council and the (then) Depart-ment for Education and Skills (DfES). These were then reproduced by the DfE (2010, pp6–26) and are highlighted below.

Effective communication and engagement with children and families:

- Listening and building empathy

- Summarising and explaining

- Consulting and negotiating
- Understanding how communication works
- Sources of support
- Importance of respect
- Identifying transition and providing support
- Understanding how children respond to change
- Knowing when and how to intervene

Safeguarding and promoting the welfare of the child:

- Relate, recognise and take considered action
- Communication, recording and reporting
- Personal skills
- Understanding the legal and procedural framework (HM Government, 2018a)
- Wider context of services
- Self-understanding

Multi-agency and integrating working (Children Act 2004):

- Effective communication and teamwork
- Assertiveness
- Being clear about your role and remit
- Knowing how to make queries
- Clear about procedures and working methods

Information sharing:

- Handling information
- Engagement
- Importance of sharing information
- Roles and responsibilities
- Awareness of challenges/complexities
- Awareness of laws and legislation (see Chapter 2)

Reflective task

Reflecting on the core skills suggested above for those practitioners and professionals working with families, children and young people:

- What core skills do you feel confident with?

- What knowledge and skills do you feel you need to develop?

A range of approaches to assessing young children and their families in a multi-professional context

The 2-year-old development review

The EYFS (DfE, 2021a, p18) states that 'when a child is aged between two and three, practitioners must review their progress, and provide parents and/or carers with a short, written summary of their child's development in the prime areas. This progress check must identify the child's strengths, and any areas where the child's progress is less than expected'.

The EYFS progress check at age 2 should:

- Review a child's development progress in their personal, social and emotional development, their physical development and their communication and language

- Ensure that parents have a clear idea of their child's development

- Enable practitioners and parents to understand the child's needs and plan activities to meet them

- Note areas where a child is progressing well and identify any areas where progress is less than expected

- Describe actions the setting intends to take to address any developmental concerns (including working with other professionals where appropriate).

The check should be completed by the setting that the child spends the most time in. It is a statutory requirement (by law) for the provider to share the progress check with the parent/s or whoever has parental responsibility. However, it is expected that parents will be encouraged to write a comment and contribute to the two-year progress check and share the information with the allocated health visitor. This should then link and contribute to the Healthy Child Programme two-year-review.

The Early Help Assessment (EHA), or Common Assessment Framework (CAF) (also known as e-CAF), is a shared assessment and planning framework for use across all children's services and all local authority areas in England and is linked the Children

Act 2004. Its main aim is to help the early identification of children and young people who may have additional needs and then to promote co-ordinated service provision to meet those needs.

The CAF for children and young people helps to promote multi-agency or integrated working as outlined in the Children Act 2004. All local authorities and relevant partners must take account of this guidance. The CAF is to be used by staff working in health, education, EY and childcare and other agencies such as those offering social care, youth services, the police and leisure provision.

The CAF is a key component of what was Every Child Matters (ECM): Change for Children programme (HM Government, 2004) and it identifies any child or young person's additional needs that are not being currently met. It initially had three main elements: a pre-assessment checklist; a process for undertaking the common assessment; and a standard proforma to document the assessment.

The main aim and principles as outlined in ECM (HM Government, 2004) of this assessment is that it:

- Is a process supported by a standard national approach and form

- Improves joint working and communication with other professionals

- Supports the sharing of information

- Rationalises assessments

- Aids better referrals

- Takes a holistic approach towards children's well-being

- Focusses on the child's needs and strengths

- Is simple, practical and understood by a range of professionals and agencies

- Empowers social agents (for example Local Children and Families Information Service) through a joint process

It must be noted that you should not complete a CAF (or EHA) without gaining consent from parents as this is an assessment tool that needs cooperation and agreement beforehand. This is not an assessment to complete if you have safeguarding concerns. It is for identifying additional support needs only. You must follow child protection procedures if you have a safeguarding concern (HM Government, 2018a) (Table 3.2).

Reflective task

Who are the main professionals that are involved in the delivery of services within the EY?

- Research the following roles, to get a better understanding of their responsibilities and the ways you could work with them according to your professional context and complete the table below.

Professional	Role and responsibilities	What do they assess and how is it done?
The Health Visitor	Responsible for children 0–5 years within a local area. Lead the co-ordination of the Healthy Child Programme. Pro-active in Safeguarding Children. Arrange and carry out home visits. Deliver preventive programmes to the most at-risk families with young children. Proactive in promoting health and preventing ill health (Shribman and Billingham, 2009).	Children's development through the two-year development review (NHS, 2022b).
The Social Worker		
The Speech and Language Therapist		
The SENCO (Special Educational Needs Coordinator)		
Other professionals you work with		

Table 3.2   Roles and responsibilities of professionals

Reflective task

Now that you have read the chapter and gained additional insight into how you work with diverse families and with professionals from a range of disciplines, how would you respond to the case study below? We hope this will support you in consolidating your learning so far.

Case study

Katerina is 4 years old, and she has been attending nursery for a year following the family gaining refugee status during the Ukrainian war with Russia.

During the last couple of months, you have attempted to raise with her mother concerns you have about Katerina's lack of speech and language development. The nursery would like to seek specialist advice to help Katerina develop to her full potential. Katerina's mum has always refused, insisting that there is

(Continued)

(Continued)

nothing wrong except that her daughter is very sensitive and that she speaks in her first language and has not yet grasped how to speak English. She has informed you that she was referred by the health visitor to a child development clinic, however she could not take the time off work to go.

Last week you again broached the subject of Katerina perhaps having additional needs that the nursery wants to understand in order to best help her. You emphasised that you have continued concerns about Katerina's lack of speech, and that you also need some help to figure out how best to engage her. Katerina's mother has again refused to give permission for advice to be sought from the SENCO (Special Educational Needs Coordinator) or for Katerina to be observed.

How would you change your approach to parent partnership working in order to improve your relationship with Katarina's mum in order to address her needs?

Summary

This chapter discussed the historical context of working with families and raises the importance of working in partnership with parents and families. It highlights their unique and diverse structures and why it is vital to be sensitive to their individual needs. It defined integrated and multi-professional working and the importance of this is laid down through relevant legislation. The range of professionals and agencies involved in the provision of services have also been introduced and discussed. The reflective tasks have been included to extend your learning and development.

4 Leading practice

At its most basic, leadership is about how a group of people is influenced (using values and vision) to achieve a common goal.

Rodd (2013, p12)

Why is knowledge and understanding of leadership important for all practitioners and how may this impact on their practice?

This chapter examines different perspectives on leading practice. Leadership in early years settings impacts on the experiences of staff, families and children as well as the professionals that liaise with early years settings. Therefore this chapter aims to highlight the roles and responsibilities of all practitioners in how they can contribute to effective leadership in EY settings. It will further explore how Early Years (EY) practitioners can be empowered in their knowledge and skills to lead and develop effective practice.

CHAPTER OVERVIEW

In this chapter we aim to help you consider:

- What is leadership?
- What is the difference between leadership and management?
- What is leadership of practice and a quality setting?
- What is the role of the practitioner in leading practice?
- What are the values, principles and visions when leading practice?
- What are some of the challenges and barriers faced when leading practice?

You will find that Chapters 2, 3, 6, 7 and 8 link closely to the topics discussed within this chapter.

This chapter links to the relevant criteria for:

Early Years Educator (Department for Education and National College for Teaching and Leadership, 2019)

- 4.1 Demonstrate a good command of the English language in spoken and written form;

- 4.2 Explain the importance of continued professional development to improve own skills and early years practice;

- 4.3 Engage in continuing professional development and reflective practice to improve own skills, practice and subject knowledge;

- 5.7 Carry out risk assessment and risk management in line with policies and procedures;

- 5.9 Maintain accurate and coherent records and reports and share information, only when appropriate, to ensure the needs of all children are met;

- 6.1 Work co-operatively with colleagues and other professionals to meet the needs of babies and children and enable them to progress;

- 6.2 Work in partnership with parents and/or carers to help them recognise and value the significant contributions they make to the child's health, well-being, learning and development.

Early Childhood Graduate Practitioner Competencies (Early Childhood Studies Degree Network, 2019)

- 3.8 Demonstrate how to promote health and educate children and families about health-related matters;

- 4.7 Identify and apply pedagogical knowledge of how to develop enabling environments indoors and outdoors;

- 5.3 Appreciate the importance of working with others to safeguard and promote the well-being of infants and young children;

- 5.7 Know when to signpost to other services or designated persons within the setting to secure young children's safeguarding and protection;

- 6.1 Evidence knowledge and understanding and application in practice of pedagogy that supports inclusion;

- 7.2 Demonstrate in practice the co-construction of learning in respectful partnership with parents and/or caregivers;

- 8.2 Apply collaborative skills in practice, including effective listening and working as a member of a team and in multi-professional contexts;

(Continued)

(Continued)

- 8.3 Demonstrate an understanding of the barriers to work with others and how to address these in practice;

- 9.4 Draw on research to demonstrate knowledge of leadership and management and its importance and application in democratic and inclusive practice;

Leadership in the context of Early Years practice

The context of our discussions in relation to leadership and management includes all EY provisions whether they are led and managed by a childminder, a nursery manager or a children centre lead. Many of these settings have an obligation to be governed. Governance of settings may use slightly different terminologies, such as being called a governing board, management group, management committee or group of trustees (Independent Commission on Good Governance in Public Services, 2005).

Leaders and managers of settings hold positions of responsibility and autonomy, and a wide range of staff rely on them to make professional judgements. Therefore, supporting staff, children, families and other professionals effectively are seen as integral to their leadership role in providing good-quality provision and services. Children Centres, for example, are underpinned by ideas relating to social justice and achievement for all children particularly those from the most deprived communities (Male and Ince, 2021).

Settings often have their own structural hierarchies. Whether they are a Children Centre, Nursery Class or School, Play Group, or Day Nursery, they will have a unique leadership and management structure in place which suits their individual circumstances. You may find, for example, in a day nursery there is a nursery manager, deputy manager, third in charge, Special Educational Needs Coordinator (SENCO), and several room leaders.

Governance arrangements

For those who may not be familiar with governance arrangements, these relate to settings' structures and organisational arrangements put in place. Governance relates to functions such as the making, implementation and monitoring of policies, and financing. Accountability for public funds such as the 2-, 3- and 4-year-old funding (GOV.UK, 2022a) is also part of their remit. Good governance and accountability are essential to meet the setting's overall purpose and objectives in an ethical manner especially where they have access to public funding.

Each setting will also have their own governance arrangements depending on whether they are a school setting or a private provider. For statutory providers such as schools these will have legal implications. It is important that you are aware of the type of governance arrangement in place within your own setting and how they operate. Their makeup will include stakeholders from a variety of people including staff, parents, local authority and community members.

Reflective task

* Who are considered leaders in your early childhood setting?
* Write down in your reflective journal your ideas and thoughts.

What is leadership and what is management?

From our experience as tutors students are often confused when asked who leads or who manages within the setting. Many will say it is the manager of the setting or the head teacher within a school environment. When we spend time in class with students, unpicking what we really mean by a leader and a manager, the common answer revolves around the roles and responsibilities people have, or the jobs they carry out or do. Rodd (2013, p19) helps to clarify a general distinction between the two roles and highlights that, 'Leaders lead people in ways that empower and develop others [whereas] Managers manage functions, processes, and people'. Leadership and management are not functions that only named leaders or managers of settings partake in. As practitioners, students or professionals, it is important to highlight that you are leading in your own right in the roles you undertake, and the responsibilities you take on. This may be leading a group of children, a room of practitioners, a parents' forum, or an outing for the children. However, many practitioners do not see themselves as leaders or are uncomfortable with the notion of being a leader (Aubrey, 2012). Male and Ince (2021) refer to the many actors who contribute to leadership roles within settings. We must be clear what the differences are between 'formal and informal leadership'; leadership responsibilities lay with those who are 'formally accountable' (Male and Ince, 2021, p390).

Rodd (2013) is clear that leadership has a great deal to do with vision and how you influence others and stresses that everyone should get involved and engaged with the many leadership opportunities that arise as part of the day-to-day running of the setting. Leadership and management are seen as integral and are very much linked together. Therefore, it is difficult to lead without managing and manage without leading (Rodd, 2006).

Role of the setting leader or manager

In relation to roles and responsibilities, 'leaders make decisions and managers operationalise those decisions' (Male and Ince, 2021, p394). Within all settings there will be a named leader or manager who will have particular responsibilities including, as discussed above, legal obligations as the person accountable for the effectiveness of the setting. All leaders and managers have a duty of care in promoting the well-being of children, staff and those attending the setting (Health and Safety Executive, 2022).

In addition, they have a responsibility for ensuring that they grow future leaders and create opportunities for staff to develop leadership skills. Delegating (and not dumping on or burdening staff) is key to supporting and developing these skills. Distributed leadership is one way of encouraging potential in staff and being proactive in helping to develop their knowledge and growing expertise in certain areas (Western, 2008). Rodd (2013) supports distributed leadership as a way of integrating both formal and informal leadership roles. In addition, this helps to encourage leadership potential and is a proactive way of developing and growing expertise in certain areas, for example, as a Designated Safeguarding Lead (DSL) or SENCO, key person, room leader or deputy manager.

Maintaining and developing quality and standards within the setting is also a part of the leader or manager's main responsibilities, and this includes eliciting contributions and feedback from a wide range of stakeholders. These stakeholders often include children, parents, practitioners, visitors and local government. The leader of the setting is responsible for the quality of provision and practice. Therefore, if the leader is the quality protector, we must agree that their influence will be significant to the quality of the setting. This idea is supported by Robins and Callan (2009) who point out that there is often a correlation between the quality of the setting and its leadership. It is clear that leaders and managers will be held responsible and accountable for the quality of their services and provision, particularly through Ofsted inspections, governors, parents and local authorities (Spencer and Dubiel, 2014). They will also be held accountable for implementing the Early Years Foundation Stage (EYFS) (DfE, 2021a) as the mandatory curriculum.

It is the leader or manager's role to formally encourage effective partnership working with parents (as discussed in Chapter 3) and you may ask why this is important. What we know from research is that parental involvement in EY settings and schools has a positive effect on children's achievement and this is one of the reasons why it must be supported (Desforges and Abouchaar, 2003; Sylva et al., 2004). Helping staff to work effectively with parents is usually a priority for any leader or manager of the setting.

Reflective task

- What is your definition or understanding of a quality provision and what role does the setting leader or manager play in developing quality provision?

- What role do practitioners play in maintaining, developing or leading quality provision?

Supporting Continuous Professional Development (CPD) and ensuring that all staff are supported and enabled to fulfil their roles and responsibilities is a key aspect of leadership and management. It is crucial to identify staff training needs and put in place development plans and opportunities, for example, by attending specific courses or through in-house peer support. These training or development needs are often identified during appraisals or through ongoing staff supervision. It also is a requirement of the EYFS (DfE, 2021a). CPD is discussed more broadly in Chapter 9.

For those of you who are unfamiliar with appraisals, in this context the word 'appraisal' implies making a judgement about how well a member of staff is doing. However, the appraisal process needs to be more than simply scoring or judging past performance. It is an annual discussion between you and your appraiser (usually your line manager). The meeting gives the staff member (appraisee) the opportunity to reflect on their work, discuss career aspirations and to identify any training needs in order to improve their practice. Feedback is generally given on their performance in a way that is constructive and motivational. At the end of the discussion, it should result in an effective personal development plan for the staff member.

Most effective settings will have an appropriate appraisal system in place that helps staff feel that their work is recognised and that they are valued. It can also provide the opportunity to discuss any areas to develop or difficulties they may have and to come up with solutions. It is a useful tool in which to focus on your performance and which you can discuss in confidence.

Throughout the year regular opportunities for reflection and one-to-one supervision contribute and link into an effective appraisal process. This will be discussed in more detail within Chapter 6 on The Importance of Assessed Practice.

Reflective task

Reflect on your last appraisal.

- Was it a useful and positive experience? If not, why not?
- If it was a positive experience, what do you believe contributed to this?
- What were your strengths and what areas were highlighted for development?

Practitioners as room leaders

Most room leaders within the nursery are often more experienced practitioners who have been given additional responsibilities. This is supported by Rodd's (2013) view that experienced practitioners generally aspire to develop their leadership skills as room leaders which helps to enhance and accelerate future career prospects.

The room leader would be expected to support the team and engage in reflective practice which leads to change and improvement. John (2019, p7) draws on the writings of Freire (1970/1986) emphasising that 'it is not enough that we reflect in order to know or understand, it is necessary to reflect in order to make a difference – to bring about change'. It is important for room leaders to help staff challenge and develop their reflections, thinking, understanding and practice in collaboration with the deputy or manager (Kitto and Bullough, 2021).

Practitioners as leaders and leadership of practice

What is the role of the practitioner in leading practice?

Leadership of practice can mean different things to different people. This chapter focusses on practice within the setting which includes how practitioners lead and support what children do, how they are encouraged and enabled. It is also about effective planning in order to meet children's individual needs, reviewing and evaluating provision. In addition, it involves how practitioners engage with, and include parents in their children's learning and development. Leading practice requires engaging in critical thinking and therefore cannot be separated from reflective practice (Bolton, 2014; Moon, 2013). When thinking about leading practice, the key is that children are central to every decision being made. This links to one of the values we hold as practitioners and leaders within EY for all children to be able to reach their full potential (Rodd, 2013; Unicef, 1989).

A leader of practice should be aware of the impact they have on others, for example, on children, their families and their professional colleagues. It is therefore crucial for the leader to model best practice in all their interactions with stakeholders. In this sense every practitioner has the potential to be an effective leader of practice.

Practitioners should be encouraged and support to see themselves as leaders in their own right. This includes leading on specific tasks and projects within the setting, for example, supporting healthy eating or carrying out risk assessments. For those of you who are not familiar with what a risk assessment is, it is a legal requirement and often links to the settings Health and Safety Policy and Procedure. Risk assessments help to support arrangements particularly for children who may have a disability or food allergy. It is important to note that the EYFS (DfE, 2021a, p37) states that 'providers must ensure that they take all reasonable steps to ensure staff and children in their care are not exposed to risks and must be able to demonstrate how they are managing risks'. These are leadership responsibilities at all levels.

Enabling environments are led and managed by practitioners where they create spaces for children that keep them safe, secure and where they can flourish and develop in an environment that is warm, supportive and welcoming. Working in partnership with parents who know their children best enables practitioners to fulfil their responsibilities as a key person for the child. Within this context children can feel more secure (Rodd, 2006).

Although the key person role is briefly discussed in Chapter 3, the responsibilities of this position are considered in more detail within this section. We also focus on the impact of the key person's role in relation to leadership and leadership of practice. In accordance with the EYFS (DfE, 2021a), every child attending an EY setting must be assigned a named key person usually a practitioner. The key person takes responsibility and leads on providing the care and learning which is specific for meeting that child's individual needs. These will include planning for their care, learning and development, observing and assessing the child, meeting regularly with the parent/s to discuss how the child is progressing and planning and agreeing next steps in their development. Where you may feel that the child has a specific educational need (SEN) ensuring that the relevant referral procedures are adhered to in conjunction with their parent/s. The referral process may bring you into contact with a range of professionals (as discussed in Chapter 3), for example, the health visitor, social worker, educational psychologist, or general practitioner. These various aspects of the key person role have the potential of developing leadership skills. For instance, by being reflective, self-aware and confident in their interactions with others.

Experienced practitioners may be asked to support students who attend placement by becoming their mentors – helping them to settle into the life of the setting, to develop professional skills on their journey in becoming a competent practitioner. Again, this is an opportunity for practitioners to improve their own leadership and management skills. When students attend settings, they are expected to be professional, and the team of practitioners are expected to support students in developing their practice. Examples of developing professional practice will include the following.

- Students are expected to be punctual and reliable, getting involved with the day-to-day activities of the setting. This will include reviewing the day with their mentor and making plans for the next day or session. It would help students if they could get involved with the wider life of the setting, for example, attending any training opportunities or celebrations.

- Students are required to inform the setting as early as possible on the day if they will be unable to attend, for example, due to an illness or family emergency. Keeping accurate details of when students attend the setting would be part of the mentor's role. Students are often required to attend for a set number of days during their individual course.

- Initially (until the student is more confident) supporting the student in organising activities. This will include ensuring that relevant resources and activity plans are prepared in advance.

- Ensuring that students adhere to equal opportunities when working with both children and adults.

- It is important for practitioners and mentors to gradually support students to take responsibility for small groups of children. They should also support students when opportunities arise to work with individual children.

- Students will be looking at their mentor as a role model and will often copy or simulate what they do. Campbell-Barr and Leeson (2016, p70) speak of the bottom-up approach to quality and the importance of 'creating and supporting effective bottom-up accountability' within all staff.

- Students are expected to be aware of any dress code the setting has. They should dress appropriately in accordance with the dress code. If there are any issues with this policy the student should speak with their mentor or visiting tutor.

- Mentors would be expected to make time to discuss the students' progress identifying areas of strength and areas that need development. They are also expected to meet with the allocated visiting tutor to discuss the students' progress.

It is important that practitioners see themselves as leaders, taking on leadership roles such as being a mentor for students and developing their own leadership and management skills. Rodd (2013, p29) conveys this when she says that 'everyone has the potential to become a leader, and everyone can learn and develop the qualities and skills required for effective leadership'.

Reflective task

You have been in your setting for a number of years and have supported several students within the setting and thinking about moving towards a more substantive leadership position within or outside of your immediate work setting. Using the following headings below, make a list of the qualities and skills you already have and/or skills you need to develop for planning your next steps.

1. Experience

2. Qualification

3. Practical skills

4. Personal qualities and attributes

In preparation for future leadership positions, many experienced practitioners have taken up the role of SENCO (DfE, 2021a). They may have applied through a formal process and therefore have a specific job description or not. However, they will often be seen as a senior member of the team (with additional pay for the responsibility) leading on the following:

- Liaising with parents and other professionals in respect of the child/ren with SEN.

- Advising and supporting other practitioners within the setting.

- Ensuring that Individual Education Plans (IEPs) or Education, Health and Care (EHC) plan is in place where applicable.

- Ensuring that relevant background information about individual children with special educational needs is collected, recorded and updated.

- Making applications to the Early Years Inclusion Panel (EYIP) (may differ according to the local authority) about individual children with more complex special educational needs.

- They will keep a profile of children with special educational needs.

- Observe and support children as appropriate on the special educational needs profile.

- Support and advise the key person, learning support assistants and other relevant staff on how to include and meet children's needs in the setting.

- Liaise with other professionals from outside services and external agencies, for example, educational psychologists, occupational therapists, physiotherapists, and speech and language therapists.

- Arrange, organise and review support for individual children.

- Keep relevant staff up to date with Special Educational Needs and Disability (SEND) and inclusion issues and to encourage personal development through courses.

- Meet with parents regularly in order to maintain good relationships and to keep parents informed about their child's progress.

- Be aware of and inform the staff team of any changes in legislation or practice from the government and the local authority.

- To review individual children's IEPs or EHC plans regularly.

- Write detailed education reports about individual children for other professionals and parents.

(DfE, 2022a)

What are the values, principles and visions when leading practice?

What are values?

Values are what we have developed during our lives. They are the ideals we live by and what we feel are important to us. For example, the importance of fairness, equality and inclusion in our work and our practice. Inclusion is based upon the idea of allowing everyone equal access to services or activities regardless of race, class, gender, sexuality, disability or religion. Values can develop and change over time, as we take in new knowledge, understanding and through our experiences.

One of the attributes of a leader is that their core beliefs inspire others. In his book Nelson Mandela (1994, p622) wrote: 'No one is born hating another person because of the colour of his skin, or his background, or his religion. People must learn to hate, and if they can learn to hate, they can be taught to love, for love comes more naturally to the human heart than its opposite' and this is an inspiration to advocate for inclusive practice.

The impact of the Equality Act 2010 determines how you must act in order to prevent and address discrimination when you provide services to the public. Discrimination, whether intentional or not, limits the settings ability to get the best from its employees. In Chapter 8 we discuss forms of discrimination in more detail.

Dickins (2014, p125) argues that 'a distributive and consultative model of leadership is the best model for supporting and developing inclusive practice'. Distributed leadership allows all members of the team to be able to contribute to its progress and the cultural norms of the setting. Therefore, effective leadership and management are crucial for the embedding of inclusive practice and must be seen as accountable for it (DfE, 2021a; Moyles, 2006; Ofsted, 2005).

Reflective task

- How do you, your leader or manager support equality and inclusion in your setting?

- Can you identify any potential or actual areas of discrimination in your setting?

- How are you going to challenge them? List your action points. Journal your reflections and responses.

Principles

A principle is very much linked to our beliefs or moral code. It is what we do with our values like a to-do or check list for treating everyone equally and fairly according to their individual needs. Having principles in leadership is closely aligned to morals and ethics which Rodd (2013) suggests are often used interchangeably.

You may be familiar with some basic principles that should guide and be embedded when working with children. We see these in the EYFS (DfE, 2021a), where there is reference to four specific principles.

1. We need to recognise that every child is a **unique child** and who is constantly learning and can be resilient, capable, confident and self-assured.

2. We need to support children who learn to be strong and independent through the many **positive relationships** that they develop.

3. We must remember that children learn and develop well in **enabling environments** with teaching and support from adults, who respond to their individual interests and needs and help them to build their learning over time. Children benefit from a strong partnership between practitioners and parents and/or carers.

4. We must put high importance on **learning and development**. Children develop and learn at different rates.

What is a vision and why is it important for those leading within EY?

A vision is the ability to look ahead at what you would like to create or something to be like. Many of us have a vision about what our own or our children's futures could or will be like or what we would like our settings to look like for the children who attend. In relation to the latter, we must see vision as 'a catalyst for action' (Rodd, 2013, p27) which prompts us to make the vision a reality.

Carter and Nutbrown (2014, pp132, 133) support the importance of values and visions stating that, 'It is crucial that early childhood educators are supported in articulating their own personal vision of early experiences for children'. Leaders of settings must also convey and discuss their vision, what they plan on doing and why, if not, this can be extremely demoralising for the staff they lead (Kouzes and Posner, 2017). Where leadership is effective practitioners have their voice and opinions heard and are able to articulate their visions. What you want in the end is a shared vision that all staff members (and other stakeholders where appropriate) are committed to.

Reflective task

- What has been your own experience of contributing to the building of a shared vision within the setting?

- What do you think it is like for those who are excluded from this important process?

- How can everyone play a part in sharing the vision of the setting? How would children be consulted?

What are some of the challenges and barriers faced when leading practice?

It is important to recognise there will be many challenges for all involved in leading practice. As highlighted by Woodrow (2008, in Baldock et al., 2013, p132) 'leadership is complex and to be effective leaders, practitioners need to develop the characteristics associated with a leadership identity'. This includes the development of emotional intelligence, which is the ability 'to identify and respond sensitively to the feelings of oneself and others' (Rodd, 2013, p58). Other common challenges have been highlighted below:

- Coping with the many changes in EY and support services.

- Maintaining commitment, motivation and energy levels among staff and preventing burn-out in the team.

- Dealing with conflict (with the different stakeholders, particularly staff).

- Developing and empowering staff through delegation, appropriate staff supervision, peer mentoring, training and continuous professional development.

- Maintaining a positive perspective when working with social disadvantage, challenging behaviours or staff distress.

- Maintaining focus on the ultimate vision to improve outcomes for children.

- Improving performance – Research is clear that good quality supports better outcomes for children (Mathers et al., 2014).

Reflective task

The quality of the setting is key to many of challenges highlighted above. Reflect on your current setting.

- Whom do you see as responsible for providing quality and why?

- How could parents influence the development of quality within the setting?

- How do or can you contribute to developing quality in your setting?

- Get a copy of your settings' most recent Ofsted inspection. Go through it highlighting the good things that contribute to developing a quality provision. Then highlight the areas for further development.

- What areas do you see as a priority to improve first within the setting and why?

Summary

This chapter discusses definitions and perspectives relating to leadership, management and practice in its broadest sense relating to all who have formal and informal leadership positions within EY. It considers the many 'actors' (Male and Ince, 2021) involved with leading practice and the importance of practitioners developing their own leadership skills and expertise. The importance of a quality setting and how this is often linked to the quality and effectiveness of the formal leader in the setting is highlighted. Distributed leadership is recognised as an effective leadership model within EY. Opportunities for reflection on issues relating to leadership offer guidance in developing your own leadership expertise and values. We emphasise that every practitioner can and should see themselves as leaders of practice within a framework of continuous professional development. Finally, we briefly consider some of the challenges and barriers faced within a range of leadership roles.

5　Effective safeguarding

Safeguarding in the 21st century means both protecting children from harm and preventing that harm from recuring, or from happening in the first place.

(Horwath and Platt, 2019, p10)

Why is knowledge and understanding of safeguarding and child protection important for all professionals and what might effective practice look like?

Everyone who comes into contact with children and families has a role to play in keeping children safe and protected (HM Government, 2018a). This chapter will offer insight into the scope of safeguarding in early childhood practice, and for the reader to gain an awareness of safeguarding practice within Early Years (EY) and Key Stage 1 (KS1) settings. The aim of this chapter is to discuss key principles which underpin statutory guidance in safeguarding and child protection. It also considers how practitioners and students can promote children's welfare and pays particular attention to specific roles and responsibilities which includes that of the Designated Safeguarding Lead (DSL) (DfE, 2021a). We will discuss why safeguarding and child protection policies and procedures are vital to effective safeguarding practice in EY settings. Key legislation such as the Children Act 1989 and Children Act 2004 will be examined in relation to safeguarding children. The role of Safeguarding Children Partnerships will be explored to further your understanding of safeguarding and child protection within your local context.

CHAPTER OVERVIEW

In this chapter we help you to consider:

- What is safeguarding and what is child protection?

- What is child abuse and its impact on development and learning?

- The role of the practitioner and student in safeguarding children

- The history of safeguarding children in the UK context

You will find that Chapters 1, 2, and 8 link closely to the topics discussed within this chapter.

This chapter links to the relevant criteria for:

Early Years Educator (Department for Education and National College for Teaching and Leadership, 2019)

- 2.10 Understand when a child is in need of additional support.

- 5.1 Know the legal requirements and guidance on health and safety, security, confidentiality of information, safeguarding and promoting the welfare of children.

- 5.2 Identify and act upon own responsibilities in relation to health and safety, security, confidentiality of information, safeguarding and promoting the welfare of children.

- 5.4 Understand why health and well-being is important for babies and children and promote healthy lifestyles.

- 5.8 Understand safeguarding policies and procedures, including child protection, recognise when a child is in danger or at risk of abuse and know how to act to protect them.

- 5.9 Maintain accurate and coherent records and reports and share information, only when appropriate, to ensure the needs of all children are met.

- 6.1 Work co-operatively with colleagues and other professionals to meet the needs of babies and children and enable them to progress.

Early Childhood Graduate Practitioner Competencies (Early Childhood Studies Degree Network, 2019)

- 5.1 Know the wider legislative and statutory guidance for safeguarding including child protection, whistle blowing, digital safety and how these are articulated into setting policy.

- 5.2 Recognise when a child may be in danger or at risk of serious harm and the procedures that must be followed.

- 5.3 Appreciate the importance of working with others to safeguard and promote the well-being of infants and young children.

(Continued)

(Continued)

- 5.4 Evidence advanced knowledge about child abuse, the wider theoretical perspectives about the causes of abuse and the potential implications for young children's outcomes.

- 5.7 Know when to signpost to other services or designated persons within the setting to secure young children's safeguarding and protections.

- 7.1 Evidence understanding of the importance of partnership with parents and/or caregivers in their role as infants and young children's first educators.

- 8.1 Evidence knowledge about the importance of creating successful, respectful professional relationships with colleagues and other professionals in and outside the setting.

- 9.5 Recognise and evidence the importance of communicating effectively orally and in writing to others.

This chapter may bring up difficult and challenging issues as we consider practice relating to safeguarding children in early childhood. While everyone has a responsibility to keep children safe and protected, as an EY professional your role entails working with families whose well-being and safety may need to be safeguarded. Becoming knowledgeable and developing competence in how to address safeguarding issues may bring up issues from your personal experience or that of someone close to you. It is important that you know how to access relevant support, and we have included some links to organisations that you can turn to at the end of this chapter.

The reflective tasks within this chapter will help you to engage with key legislation and guidance such as: What to do if you're worried a child is being abused, Advice for practitioners (HM Government, 2015) and Working Together to Safeguard Children (WTSC) (HM Government, 2018a) and we advise you to download these documents from the UK government website as we will referring to these throughout.

In the context of this chapter, safeguarding relates to practice in early childhood and KS1 settings that seeks to promote the welfare of children and protect children from harm. Safeguarding practice in England for early childhood settings and schools is guided by the Statutory Framework of the Early Years Foundation Stage (EYFS) (DfE, 2021a) and Keeping children safe in education 2022 (DfE, 2022b) respectively. Both guiding documents are informed by the statutory guidance WTSC (HM Government, 2018a). 'Statutory' refers to what is required by Acts of Parliament. For example, the learning and development as well as the safeguarding and welfare requirements of the EYFS are underpinned by sections 39 (1) (a) and 39 (1) (b) of the Childcare Act 2006 (DfE, 2021a).

What is safeguarding and what is child protection?

In line with WTSC document, safeguarding children means

- 'protecting children from maltreatment

- preventing impairment of children's mental and physical health or development ensuring that children grow up in circumstances consistent with the provision of safe and effective care

- taking action to enable all children to have the best outcomes'

(HM Government, 2018a, p7) and informs this chapter. It makes clear, safeguarding requires practitioners to take action and be proactive (Horwath and Platt, 2019).

Child protection focusses on individual children, who have been identified as likely to suffer or suffering significant harm (NSPCC, 2022a). It is important to differentiate between safeguarding and child protection, according to the legislation underpinning safeguarding children in England. The Children Act 1989 introduced the concept of 'children in need' (Section 17) and distinguishes this from children who are at risk of 'significant harm' and in need of protection (Section 47).

Section 17 of the Children Act 1989 puts a duty on every local authority 'to safeguard and promote the health and welfare of children in need within their area'. A child in need is defined by the Children Act 1989 as a child

- who is unlikely to achieve or maintain a reasonable standard of health and development without the provision of local authority services.

- whose health and development is likely to be significantly impaired without the provision of local authority services.

- who is disabled.

According to Section 47 of the Children Act 1989, where significant harm is suspected or identified, the local authority must intervene to protect a child. An important clarification was made in the Adoption and Children Act 2002, which defined significant harm as 'seeing or hearing the ill-treatment of another'. This would be, for example, when a child witnesses a parent being subjected to 'physical acts of violence' as may be the case in domestic abuse (HM Government, 2018a, p10).

Section 31 of the Children Act 1989 defines harm as the 'ill treatment or the impairment of the health or development of the child', and harm is determined as significant when 'comparing a child's health and development with what might be reasonably expected of a similar child'. This definition may seem vague, and as determining significant harm relies on the referral to and judgement made by local authorities' social services, police, education or health agencies (NSPCC, 2022b), it is vital that practitioners at the frontline working with children and families have a secure understanding of what accounts as child abuse.

What is child abuse?

The current WTSC guide defines child abuse as 'a form of maltreatment of a child' and this includes 'failing to act to prevent harm' (HM Government, 2018a, p106). It stresses this includes harm done as a result from witnessing maltreatment of others, for example, where abuse happens to other household or family members. It emphasises harm may result from physical as well as other forms of ill-treatment and includes online abuse or harm done offline but enabled through use of technology. The WTSC document recognises abuse is more likely to happen to children from people known to them within the family, institutions or community settings, and makes clear an abuser may be an adult or adults, a child or children (HM Government, 2018a).

To be able to respond to abuse and neglect, practitioners need to be alert to and recognise observable signs and symptoms of abuse. The next task asks you to engage with key documents to develop a secure understanding how abuse and neglect may present itself.

Reflective task

Go online and download the guidance document by HM Government (2015) What to do if you're worried a child is being abused, Advice for practitioners.

- Read each of the signs and symptoms of abuse on page 6 of the document.

- Reflect on these and consider any cases where you may have been worried about a child. What action did you take?

- Have you been surprised by any of the signs listed? Reflect why these may have been listed here.

Child abuse is generally distinguished between four main categories of physical, emotional, sexual abuse and neglect. Table 5.1 draws on two key government documents defining each of these types of abuse how it may be noticed in children's behaviour or appearance. As outlined in the government guidance for practitioners 'the warning signs and symptoms of child abuse and neglect can vary from child to child' and recognising abuse and neglect can be challenging for practitioners working with children and their families (HM Government, 2015, p5). Indication of abuse and neglect may be observed in the child, the parents or both. While practitioners need to be alert to these and know how to respond, judgement of what the appropriate response will ultimately be is made by the relevant local authority children's social care.

Types of abuse	Definitions of abuse according to working together to safeguard children 2018 (HM Government, 2018a)	Signs and symptoms of abuse According to what to do if you're worried a child is being abused (HM Government, 2015)
Physical abuse	• Includes 'hitting, shaking, throwing, poisoning, burning or scalding, drowning, suffocating or otherwise causing physical harm to a child. [...] and • when a parent or carer fabricates the symptoms of, or deliberately induces, illness in a child'. (Adapted from HM Government, 2018a, p106)	Children may have 'frequent injuries, unexplained or unusual fractures or broken bones, and/or unexplained: • bruises or cuts; • burns or scalds; or • bite marks'. (Adapted from HM Government, 2015, p7)
Emotional abuse	• 'may involve conveying to a child that they are worthless or unloved, inadequate, or valued only insofar as they meet the needs of another person'. • 'includes not giving the child opportunities to express their views, deliberately silencing them or "making fun" of what they say or how they communicate'. • 'may feature age or developmentally inappropriate expectations being imposed on children.' • 'may involve seeing or hearing the ill-treatment of another'. • 'may involve serious bullying (including cyber bullying), causing children frequently to feel frightened or in danger, or the exploitation or corruption of children'. (Adapted from HM Government, 2018a, p107).	Children may be 'excessively withdrawn, fearful or anxious about doing something wrong' Their parents or carers • 'may withdraw their attention from their child, giving the child the 'cold shoulder'' • 'blame their problems on their child' • 'humiliate their child, for example, by name-calling or making negative comparisons'. (Adapted from HM Government, 2015, p8)
Sexual abuse	• 'involves forcing or enticing a child or young person to take part in sexual activities, not necessarily involving a high level of violence, whether or not the child is aware of what is happening.' • 'may involve physical contact, including assault by penetration (for example, rape or oral sex) or non-penetrative acts such as masturbation, kissing, rubbing and touching outside of clothing'.	Children may • 'display knowledge or interest in sexual acts inappropriate to their age' • 'use sexual language or have sexual knowledge that you wouldn't expect them to have' • 'ask others to behave sexually or play sexual games' • 'have physical sexual health problems, including soreness in the genital and anal areas, sexually transmitted infections or be pregnant underage'.

Types of abuse	Definitions of abuse according to working together to safeguard children 2018 (HM Government, 2018a)	Signs and symptoms of abuse According to what to do if you're worried a child is being abused (HM Government, 2015)
	• 'may also include non-contact activities, such as involving children in looking at, or in the production of, sexual images, watching sexual activities, encouraging children to behave in sexually inappropriate ways, or grooming a child in preparation for abuse'. (Adapted from HM Government, 2018a, p107)	(Adapted from HM Government, 2015, p8)
Neglect	• 'is the persistent failure to meet a child's basic physical and/or psycho-logical needs, likely to result in the serious impairment of the child's health or development.' • 'may occur during pregnancy as a result of maternal substance abuse.' 'Once a child is born, neglect may involve a parent or carer failing to:' • 'provide adequate food, clothing and shelter (including exclusion from home or abandonment)' • 'protect a child from physical and emotional harm or danger' • 'ensure adequate supervision (including the use of inadequate caregivers)' • 'ensure access to appropriate medical care or treatment' 'It may also include neglect of, or unresponsiveness to, a child's basic emotional needs'. (Adapted from HM Government, 2018a, p107)	Children may • live 'in a home that is indisputably dirty or unsafe' • be 'left hungry or dirty' • be 'left without adequate clothing, e.g. not having a winter coat' • be 'living in dangerous conditions, i.e. around drugs, alcohol or violence' • be 'often angry, aggressive or may self-harm' • 'fail to receive basic health care' Parents may 'fail to seek medical treatment when their children are ill or are injured'. (Adapted from HM Government, 2015, p10)

Table 5.1   Signs and symptoms of different types of abuse

Signs and symptoms of abuse

It is important to be aware that abuse can happen in any family (NSPCC, 2022c). Lumsdon (2016, p56) explains reasons why abuse happens in some families are often multi-layered and difficult to establish, but issues such as 'marital conflict, unwanted pregnancy, mental health, drug and alcohol dependency, and previous experience of abuse', or those relating to material poverty are commonly found in families where abuse happens. Particular vulnerabilities to physical abuse, for example, include being very young (such as babies and infants) or having a disability (HM Government, 2015). Neglect is likely to occur alongside other types of abuse and where drug and alcohol abuse takes place, or when a parent cannot provide the care necessary due to physical or psychological reasons (HM Government, 2015). Practitioners should also be aware that 'some level of emotional abuse is involved in all types of maltreatment of a child, though it may occur alone' (HM Government, 2018a, p107).

These circumstances are regularly referred to as adverse childhood experiences (ACE), defined as 'highly stressful, and potentially traumatic, events or situations that occur during childhood and/or adolescence, which can be a single event, or prolonged threats to, and breaches of, the young person's safety, security, trust or bodily integrity' (Young Minds and NHS England, 2018, p22). This definition makes all too clear that abuse and neglect are examples of ACE and may occur within the context of the child in the family.

Historic abuse refers to adults who have been abused as a child. The various roles practitioners hold in the setting may make them privy to personal information about parents' or carers' lives. EY practitioners need to understand that abuse can have a significant long-term impact on individuals and in turn, may affect those in close relationships with them (NSPCC, 2022d). This is an indication for all working with children and families to recognise that abuse needs an appropriate and timely response. Where historic abuse has been disclosed, practitioners should be aware a supportive and understanding response may include signposting to relevant agencies. This could be the police or agencies that provide specialist help and support for survivors of abuse.

In support of understanding abuse more comprehensively, abuse is differentiated in more detail as shown below and includes:

- Bullying (including cyber bullying)
- Child trafficking
- Child criminal exploitation and Gangs
- Child sexual exploitation
- Domestic abuse
- Female Genital Mutilation
- Grooming
- Online abuse
- Radicalisation

(HM Government, 2018a)

> ### *Reflective task*
>
> Download the following documents and use these to inform yourself of the different types of abuse listed above
>
> *   Working Together to Safeguard Children (HM Government, 2018a)
> *   What to do if you're worried a child is being abused (HM Government, 2015)
> *   Keeping children safe in education 2022 (DfE, 2022b) (if you are working in a school)
> *   Write your own definition of each of these types of abuse, then reflect and note in your reflective journal why you think it is important for practitioners to be knowledgeable about these forms of abuse. Share your reflections with your mentor or visiting tutor.

The role of the practitioner and student in safeguarding children

Safeguarding children in England happens within a multi-disciplinary and multi-agency framework based on the Children Act 1989 and Children Act 2004 and is carried out at local authority level. Multi-disciplinary working requires a range of professionals with particular areas of expertise to work together to address specific safeguarding concerns and to protect a child or children from harm. It means relevant agencies, for example, from education (including EY), health, housing, police working together to apply a 'coordinated approach' (HM Government, 2018a, p11). Terms such as inter-agency working may also be used in key government documents relating to safeguarding children.

The significance of cooperation and partnership working to protect children from harm and safeguarding their welfare is highlighted in the title of the WTSC document and demonstrated by the requirement for local authorities to establish local safeguarding partnerships. The three local safeguarding partners (LSP) are the local authority, police and clinical commissioning group (health) (HM Government, 2018a). Settings' safeguarding policy should reflect guidance and procedures of the relevant LSP (DfE, 2021a). While these arrangements have been established in line with WTSC document to strengthen safeguarding practice at local level, alarmingly, these changes have not yet been effectively implemented across the country. This was evidenced by the national review into the murders of Arthur Labinjo-Hughes and Star Hobson, which found 'multi-agency arrangements for protecting children are more fractured and fragmented than they should be' (The Child Safeguarding Practice Review Panel, 2022, p10).

The role of the designated safeguarding lead (DSL)

One of the key roles with specific responsibilities in relation to safeguarding children in early childhood settings is the designated lead for safeguarding. Statutory guidance (DfE, 2021a; DfE, 2022b) stipulates for providers to have a named designated safeguarding lead (DSL), whose role it is 'to support other practitioners in their organisations and agencies to recognise the needs of children, including protection from possible abuse or neglect' (HM Government, 2018a, p59). The DSL is responsible for addressing concerns regarding the well-being and safety of children and works jointly with local statutory children's services, agencies and their Local Safeguarding Children Partnership (LSCP). All staff including student practitioners need to know who the DSL for the setting is. DSLs are required to have child protection training which allows them to support staff in their safeguarding duties. However, safeguarding does not rest with the DSL, but all who work in early childhood settings. It is required that all practitioners are knowledgeable about the settings' safeguarding policy and procedures and aware of current safeguarding issues' (DfE, 2021a).

Sharing information

It is crucial that practitioners are knowledgeable about their roles and responsibilities to support effective collaboration between professionals and relevant agencies. For example, as a key person (DfE, 2021a) you may hold essential information about a child in your care, which on its own may not seem relevant, but when put together with information from other agencies or professionals may prove significant in identifying safeguarding concerns. Think of this process as completing a puzzle, with each individual who knows the child holding one specific piece of the puzzle, which could include information about the child or the family. Only when all pieces are laid down, a clear picture of the case emerges. This image also helps to see the potential value of each piece of information in order to overcome barriers that may prevent practitioners sharing information. For example, practitioners or students may be fearful of sharing information, or they may not appreciate the relevance of the information they hold. Where practitioners are aware that within the context of safeguarding children, the General Data Protection Regulation (GDPR) and Data Protection Act 2018 do not present a barrier to sharing information, they are more likely to share potentially relevant information (HM Government, 2018b).

The EYFS helps practitioners to recognise 'inappropriate behaviour displayed by other members of staff, or any other person working with the children, for example: inappropriate sexual comments; excessive one-to-one attention beyond the requirements of their usual role and responsibilities; or inappropriate sharing of images' (DfE, 2021a, p22). Every setting's safeguarding and child protection policy must outline the procedures to follow when allegations of abuse or neglect are made against any staff. Effective implementation of the setting's safeguarding policy means practitioners understand the role of the Local Authority Designated Officer (LADO) who 'manages and has an oversight of allegations made against people who work with children' and follow the settings procedure where a referral has been made (HM Government, 2018a, p109). The role of the DSL is particularly relevant here, as referrals to the LADO (with the exception of the allegation being made against the DSL) will be made by the DSL.

It is the Office for Standards in Education, Children's Services and Skills' (Ofsted) role to regulate and inspect early childhood and school provision. As part of this, they make judgements on the effectiveness of the setting's safeguarding arrangements with serious consequences where these have been judged as being ineffective or requiring improvement (Ofsted, 2022a). Where required improvements as outlined by Ofsted are not made within a given time frame, the setting may have to close. Effective setting policy will need to include the relevant contact details of Ofsted, who will need to be informed within 14 days of an allegation being made for example against a staff member (Ofsted, 2022b).

Recording safeguarding concerns

Recognising safeguarding concerns relies on all practitioners being observant and to understand when to record, share information and with whom. Setting policies should outline procedures regarding note taking, such as the need for these to be dated, signed and legible. Observations should be detailed, and non-judgemental in cases where a child, or their carer discloses a safeguarding concern or is showing concerning behaviour (e.g., being under the influence of drugs, or being verbally abusive). What is recorded should reflect any spoken words as closely as possible. Procedures regarding the storage of information need to be appropriate to the high level of confidentiality warranted regarding the disclosure of any safeguarding concerns. In addition, policy must be clear when and how the DSL will be informed, and alternative processes outlined if for any reason the DSL cannot be informed or contacted.

Practitioners need to be aware that young children may disclose what might be a safeguarding concern at any time and know how to respond appropriately. When a child discloses information that raises a safeguarding concern, practitioners must listen with 'compassion and understanding', their body language should be 'open and encouraging' and they should be 'respectful of pauses and don't interrupt' the child' and importantly, 'reflect back' on what the child has said, using 'their language to show it's their experience' (NSPCC, 2019). Where a setting has established a culture of listening to children as outlined in Chapter 1 of this book, this also provides a strong foundation for effective safeguarding practice.

Reflective task

Reflect on the way you have been introduced to the safeguarding policies of your setting and any additional trainings you have received.

- How confident are you with the policies and procedures regarding safeguarding practice in your setting?

- Examine in detail the setting's policies and procedures relating to safeguarding and child protection. Also look into whether there are processes with regards to whistle blowing, and how digital safety is supported through policies and procedures.

- Reflect on your experience of developing your knowledge and understanding regarding safeguarding arrangements in the setting.

- Do you feel you have been supported in getting know the safeguarding procedures? If yes, how?

- Is there anything that could be improved and why?

Supporting the well-being of the child in the family

Well-being can be considered from a range of perspectives. Heathwood's (2021, p5) philosophical outlook sees well-being as 'concerning what is basically good for us' and may bring up helpful images of what well-being may entail. Thinking of well-being of children in the family, Bronfenbrenner's (1979) ecological systems theory shows determinants to children's well-being are multi-layered and their well-being is directly influenced by their immediate family and wider community. Further, it reminds us that ACE will also impact on children's well-being as will wider societal and political influences.

Bowlby and Ainsworth's (Holmes, 2014) research led to the development of the concept of attachment which still informs today's practice in early childhood and is of particular relevance when considering children's well-being. Attachment theory places value on a child's earliest experience of their relationship with their primary caregiver (Holmes, 2014). Bowlby and Ainsworth found the way these relationships have been experienced is of significance to a child's development of attachment style, which also serves as a blueprint for future relationships (Holmes, 2014). Children's development is reliant on their carer'(s) responses to their emotional states of contentment and distress and the experience of having their needs met reliably and in a responsive way helps children to develop confidence in others (Gerhardt, 2004). For example, a securely attached child will show their emotions when distressed, assured their parent or attachment figure will meet their need for comfort and support.

Distress and discomfort are part of everyone's life experience and in most cases, being resilient serves as an important skill in managing such experiences including those caused by ACE. However, when children are subjected to maltreatment from caregivers, strengthening a child's resilience without their caregiver's support and participation is often ineffective (Shemmings and Shemmings, 2019). As part of its safeguarding and welfare requirements the EYFS stipulates a key person is assigned to each child. The keyperson will aim to build trusting relationships with the family and where appropriate, 'help them to engage with more specialist support' (DfE, 2021a, p17). The provision of early help (see Chapter 3 for more detail) is relevant here as outlined by the WTSC document. It is based on the premise that providing support early on may prevent escalation of circumstances, where action would need to be taken according to Section 17 or Section 47 of the Children Act 1989.

What is the impact of child abuse on children's learning and development?

Child abuse and neglect have an impact on a child's development overall. Naughton (2018) stresses the immense impact of children's physical and social environment on children's development, in particular the development of the brain, and the subsequent effect on children's ability to reach their full potential. A helpful theoretical concept understanding the impact of abuse and neglect is that of Maslow (1943) which is based on the view that all humans strive to reach their full potential, which he called 'self-actualisation'. Maslow saw self-actualisation at the top of a hierarchy of human basic needs. According to Maslow (1943) in order for higher needs to emerge, those lower down the hierarchy must be fulfilled. For example, 'physiological needs' such a food, shelter, sleep must be met before 'safety needs' and the need for 'love' become important. Being healthy and pro-tected, feeling that you belong and that you are loved is essential before higher needs such as 'esteem' and finally 'self-actualisation' will emerge. Maslow's (1943) hierarchy of needs is often presented as pyramid, and it may be helpful for you to find an image of this online. It will help you to understand that when children experience abuse and neglect, this may present a threat to their fundamental needs and subsequently their ability to learn, develop self-esteem confidence and per-sonal growth. All these are related to Maslow's higher needs.

Brief historical perspective on safeguarding children

'Child abuse is as old as time itself' (Moore, 2018, p15), yet what accounts as abuse is seen differently across cultures and has changed over time. Numerous historical accounts show that children have been victims of cruelty and abuse in past civili-sations, which at the time may have not been acknowledged as abuse (Frost, 2021). The legislative framework which guides safeguarding practice has been informed by the many tragic cases of child abuse and neglect. In England, a child safeguarding practice review is carried out when a child dies or is seriously harmed. This is to learn how professionals and organisations can develop practice and work together to ensure children are safeguarded more effectively in future. Such reviews may lead to significant changes made to legislation and practice and have been introduced as a result of the enquiry carried out by Lord Laming on the death of 8-year-old Victoria Climbié (GOV.UK, 2003). His enquiry led to the implementation of the Children Act 2004 and in turn resulted in the introduction of serious case reviews (now called child safeguarding practice reviews).

Reflective task

The death of 12-year-old Dennis O'Neill in 1945 led to the first formal child death enquiry in England (NSPCC, 2022e). Subsequent changes to legislation included the passing of the Children Act 1948 (Gillard, 2014) which placed a duty on local authorities to take care of orphaned children.

- Failures in safeguarding children are frequently reported in the media. Find out about a case where a child or children have been failed by the systems in place and the changes to legislation and practice that followed.

- What were the failings? Were recommendations made to avoid these in the future?

A significant milestone in the history of safeguarding children can be pinpointed to Children Act 1989 coming into force on the 14th of October 1991, closely coinciding with the United Kingdom ratifying the UNCRC (Unicef, 1989). Today's child protection system in England and Wales is still based on the Children Act 1989 and its key principles. An independent review of the child protection system in England in 2011 recommended that the child protection system should be more child-centred and reflective of the UNCRC (Munro, 2011).

Reflective task

In Chapter 1 you were asked to download the articles of the UNCRC (Unicef, 1989). Now take a look at those articles again and relate these to children's well-being, safeguarding and protection from harm and abuse.

- Reflect and write down how each of the articles supports children's welfare and protects them from harm and abuse.

The recommendations of the Munro (2011) review led to a revision of the WTSC document which was published in 2013 (DfE and Timpson, 2013). It has since been updated in 2015 and again in 2018 to its current version. The recent updates respectively respond to children's emerging needs through 'early help' (HM Government, 2018a, p13) and with the implementation of the Children and Social Work Act 2017, the introduction of local safeguarding partnerships: Local Authority, Police and Health partners, the framework we currently are working with.

Reflective task

As your final reflective task, consider now the following case study which will help you to apply your knowledge and understanding gained in this chapter.

Case Study

Marco is 4 years old and lives with his mum Talia. He has been attending your setting for the last two years. His complex health needs mean that he receives care from a range of health services. You know from Talia, that Marco's dad left them 15 months ago and rarely has had contact with Marco since. Talia's family lives abroad, and she seems to have very few local contacts. On some days when Talia brings Marco to nursery, she seems exhausted and there were occasions you could smell alcohol on her breath. In the last couple of months Marco has been frequently late and has missed some days. When he is in nursery, he get easily upset and his keyperson is unable to settle him. Staff have noticed a deterioration in his appearance. Talia did not attend the meeting arranged with Marco's keyperson and although offered, did not agree to a different date. At breakfast time today, Marco tells his key person he had no food in the evening because his mum was sleeping and did not wake up and that the lady next door put him to bed.

- What are your concerns about this child?
- What are your first actions as a practitioner?
- What are your first actions as a manager?

Discuss your responses with a colleague, mentor, tutor or another professional.

Summary

Practitioners' actions have the potential to make a difference to a child's or their family's life to ensure they are safe and protected from harm and abuse. Knowledgeable, reflective and caring practitioners are equipped to support effective safeguarding practice. They will have a sound understanding of statutory guidance, setting policies and procedures, and an awareness of how biases and attitudes may influence perceptions. They will demonstrate an empathetic response to disclosure of what may be a safeguarding concern. By engaging with the chapter's reflective tasks and the case study you will have developed knowledge and understanding of safeguarding children in the context of your role in the setting as well as a deeper understanding of the historical and political context that informs safeguarding practice today. Finally, and importantly, you will be aware that everyone has a responsibility in safeguarding children.

Organisations that offer information and advise

National Society for the Prevention of Cruelty to Children (NSPCC)

https://www.nspcc.org.uk/

- National charity working to help children to be safe from abuse

Childline

https://www.childline.org.uk/

- National Charity (part of NSPCC) helping anyone under 19 years offering a free, private and confidential service where children can talk about any issue they are going through

Women's aid

https://www.womensaid.org.uk/

- National charity aiming to end domestic abuse against women and children

Talk campus

https://www.talkcampus.io/

- Online peer support community available to students worldwide via their App

Samaritans

https://www.samaritans.org/

- National Charity aiming to prevent suicide by providing support to people who are struggling to cope and in times of crisis

Citizens advice

https://www.citizensadvice.org.uk/

- National charity offering advice for citizens on a wide range of issues

6 The importance of assessed practice

Learners decide to study Early Childhood Studies at different ages, times in their life, with different entry qualifications and reasons. Some students have considerable experience in practice, others have minimal or no experience at all. However, they share an aspiration to work with children and families.

(Early Childhood Studies Degree Network, 2019, p4)

Why is knowledge and understanding of assessed practice important for all practitioners and professionals and how can it support students in their setting placement?

This chapter guides the reader through the placement journey which students may undertake as part of developing their professional practice and which will be accredited as part of their degree as long as the student has passed the relevant criteria successfully. It aims to encourage students in placement practice to reflect on their learning and experiences. It will discuss the importance of keeping a reflective journal and how it can assist their professional development as an Early Years (EY) practitioner. We will consider the importance of student practitioners in placement developing their professional practice within the setting. Further, it will support students and practitioners in developing and strengthening the skills and attributes necessary for a successful placement experience. It encourages all practitioners to embrace core professional values and will illustrate the impact these have on practice and how they support students' professional development. The chapter offers reflective tasks as well as practical guidance to support students through their assessments of practice and explains the important role of the mentor and visiting tutor in the context of assessed practice.

CHAPTER OVERVIEW

In this chapter we help you to consider:

- The history and contexts in which early childhood practice is assessed

(Continued)

- The role of the setting mentor and visiting tutor
- The role of the student in placement
- The relevance of the placement experience
- How to develop skills of reflection and the importance of keeping a reflective journal
- How to prepare for an assessment of practice

You will find that Chapters 1, 2, 4 and 9 link closely to the topics discussed within this chapter.

This chapter links to the relevant criteria for:

Early Years Educator (Department for Education and National College for Teaching and Leadership, 2019)

- 1.9 Understand the current early education curriculum requirements.
- 1.10 Promote equality of opportunity and anti-discriminatory practice.
- 4.3 Engage in continuing professional development and reflective practice to improve own skills, practice and subject knowledge (for example, in English, Mathematics, music, history or modern foreign languages).
- 5.2 Identify and act upon own responsibilities in relation to health and safety, security, confidentiality of information, safeguarding and promoting the welfare of children.
- 5.8 Understand safeguarding policies and procedures, including child protection, recognise when a child is in danger or at risk of abuse, and know how to act to protect them.
- 5.9 Maintain accurate and coherent records and reports and share information, only when appropriate, to ensure the needs of all children are met.
- 6.1 Work co-operatively with colleagues and other professionals to meet the needs of babies and children and enable them to progress.

(Continued)

(Continued)

- 6.2 Work in partnership with parents and/or carers to help them recognise and value the significant contributions they make to the child's health, well-being, learning and development.

- 6.3 Encourage parents and/or carers to take an active role in the child's play, learning and development.

Early Childhood Graduate Practitioner Competencies (Early Childhood Studies Degree Network, 2019)

- 1.2 Observe, support and extend young children's participation in their learning through following their needs and interests.

- 4.2 Apply a range of observation and research skills to co-construct young children's development, play and learning, encouraging independence and next steps.

- 7.1 Evidence understanding of the importance of partnership with parents and/or caregivers in their role as infants and young children's first educators.

- 8.1 Evidence knowledge about the importance of creating successful, respectful professional relationships with colleagues and other professionals in and outside the setting.

History and contexts in which early childhood practice is assessed

The impact of early childhood education on outcomes for children has been demonstrated by studies such as the Effective Provision of Pre-school Education (EPPE) project (Sylva et al., 2004) and the study Researching Effective Pedagogy in the Early Years (REPEY) (Siraj-Blatchford et al., 2002). Both these studies paved the way for further government policy development impacting on the qualification levels of EY practitioners. Since 2004 government funding has been made available to ensure the development of graduate level practitioners in the EY sector. For example, the National Professional Qualification in Integrated Centre Leadership (NPQICL) helped (at that time) to develop leaders to work within Children Centres (National College for School Leadership, n.d.). Coming from a range of professions, including childcare professionals, the programme supported the development of Children Centre leaders with the skills and abilities 'to improve outcomes for vulnerable children' (National College for School Leadership, n.d., p6). The National Professional Qualification for Headship (NPQH) (GOV.UK, 2014) is the equivalent for head teachers within schools. EY practitioners educated to NVQ level 3 were able to access degree courses relating to EY and then progress to enter the workforce as graduate leaders in the sector through achieving Early Years Professional Status (EYPS) (Fitzgerald and Kay, 2016). These policy developments aimed to professionalise the EY workforce (Osgood, 2012). The goal was to achieve positive long-term outcomes for children and their families, in particular those who are affected by inequality issues such as poverty (Allen, 2011; Field, 2010).

All aspiring EY practitioners, whether on the pathway to achieve the Early Years Educator (EYE) qualification, obtain Graduate Practitioner Competencies (GPC) or become an Early Years Teacher (EYT), are required to gain practice experience as part of their professional development journey. These qualifications require students to be assessed on their practice. The consensus of assessed practice is evident on a range of professional development routes. Regarding EYE, it is the Department for Education that defines the criteria that must be met to achieve EYE, and for practitioners to demonstrate their competence accordingly (Department for Education and National College for Teaching and Leadership, 2019). The GPCs are aligned to the Quality Assurance Agency (QAA) subject benchmark statements for Early Childhood Studies. Institutions which are a member of the Early Childhood Studies Degree Network (ECSDN) (2022) may offer this professional practice option as part of the degree course for those students who fulfil the necessary entry requirements. The QAA (2022, p5) supports the inclusion of a professional practice element being integrated within ECS degree courses, stating that 'the linking of theory and practice is integral throughout the whole degree. In addition, some honours degrees encourage professional and practice development and may offer the opportunity for students to meet the requirements of particular statutory or regulatory bodies, through the structure and content of the course'. Originally recognised as EYPS, the now named Early Years Teacher Status is awarded to graduates who are leading education and care from birth to five and who have been judged to have met all the standards in practice (National College for Teaching and Leadership, 2013).

The type of settings where students may be placed in order to gain their professional practice experience include settings within the voluntary, statutory or private sector such as play groups and community nurseries, children's centres or day nurseries, reception classes or school nurseries. The EYE qualification requires students to gain experience with children aged 3–5 years as well as children from birth to three years old. Similarly, when training to achieve EYT, practice experience will be based in settings delivering the Early Years Foundation Stage (EYFS) (DfE, 2021a) such as Children Centres, private nurseries, school nurseries and reception classes. To achieve the GPC students will, in addition to showing competency within the EYFS, health or social care settings, be required to complete placement practice within the age range from birth to eight (Early Childhood Studies Degree Network, 2019).

In the following sections we consider placement experience from the viewpoint of the student, setting mentor and visiting tutor. In this way it will prepare students for their placement experience as well as providing guidance throughout the practice element of their course, including the assessment of practice. Firstly, we will outline the roles of the setting mentor and the visiting tutor.

Role of the setting mentor

As a mentor it is advisable to expect that students may have very limited experience in the field of early childhood education and care and therefore will need support and guidance during their placement. Their role is to share practice and skills, offer ideas regarding practice with children and families and brokering access to different experiences within the setting. It is important to understand students in placement will not count towards the staff to child ratios and should not be left unsupervised when working with children. To work effectively in their role, it is highly desirable that setting mentors will be experienced and skilled practitioners who have knowledge and understanding of the criteria or competency their mentee is working towards. However the mentee also has a responsibility to communicate and make information regarding EYE criteria or GPC available to their mentor. In addition, training providers may offer mentor training sessions and, in this way, distribute necessary and important information and documentation. This will support mentors to agree with their mentee the expectations regarding, for example, the level of commitment their attendance, including taking part in staff meetings, or setting events. Their role involves assessing students' practice and giving formative and, (where appropriate), summative feedback using an agreed marking criteria. Their in-depth knowledge and understanding of the setting is highly valuable when supporting students to identify relevant goals. These should be in line with their expected professional development as well as the demands set by the criteria or competencies. This works well when maintaining ongoing and regular contact with the mentee which could involve meeting at a mutually agreed time for 15–30 minutes every two weeks. These meetings have the potential to offer opportunities for mentees to develop their reflective practice. Within this context, any difficulties or challenges the mentee faces, may be identified and discussed. Mentors should encourage their mentees to resolve these for themselves, and when needed may identify and help mentees to draw on their own strengths and abilities. This will enable mentees to resolve any issues that have been identified. In order for mentees to succeed, mentors should ensure appropriate opportunities are made available. Examples of these may be: facilitating contact with parents when appropriate, or interactions with other professionals and staff as part of their provision and in line with the EYFS (DfE, 2021a). Over time the regular meetings enable review of the mentee's progress and discussion of targets for development. Depending on the processes of the training provided, this may form part of a three-way interaction with the visiting tutor.

Role of the visiting tutor

The visiting tutor is usually affiliated with and employed by the training provider. Their role is to assess the student within the placement setting according to the assessment criteria as outlined by the training provider. To carry out this role effectively, the visiting tutor should introduce themselves formally to each of the students they have been allocated to, inform them of their role and share relevant contact details. Informing the student well in advance of their first placement visit allows the student to communicate this to the setting as there could be a setting event planned which may make an assessment visit on a particular day unsuitable. Where practically possible, the visiting tutor may also meet with the students' mentor to discuss how the student has settled into the setting or to identify appropriate goals and targets. This is a good opportunity for the visiting tutor and the setting mentor to build a working relationship and identify any concerns or areas of support that need to be addressed. The visiting tutor will complete an individual learning plan with the student, and this may be part of a three-way discussion including the student, mentor and their visiting tutor. The discussion will support the student in identifying and planning their next steps and targets. Sharing a record of the discussion and agreed targets with the student allows them to plan accordingly, and helps to ensure that these targets can be monitored and followed up on the next visit. Any particular issues that need to be addressed with the student such as unexplained absences should be addressed early on and before they impact more significantly on the students' progress and placement experience. As part of their visiting role, the tutor will observe the student and help the student reflect on their practice. They should give constructive feedback to enable the student to develop their professional practice.

Aims of the placement experience

In order to achieve EYE, students usually gain placement experience over two academic years. For those developing their practice towards achieving GPC, where appropriate, they will undertake additional practice experience usually within their final year of an Early Childhood Studies degree course. For any placement experience to be meaningful and enable students to gain the relevant professional competencies successfully, the learning and development opportunities should reflect their level of study, ability and practice experience.

Ideally, the first year of placement should enable students:

- to reflect on their personal value systems and begin to develop reflective practice.
- to gain an understanding of the importance of observation and how these allow practitioners to plan, implement and reflect on activities carried out within the setting.
- to consider the professional skills required within an EY setting including communication, teamwork, partnership with parents within the context of an anti-bias approach.
- to engage with the Level 3 EYE qualifications criteria. (This can be accessed online.)

Where possible, in the second year of placement practice students will aim to

- meet the EYE criteria in full.

- continue to develop proficiency it their practice and further their skills as a critically reflective practitioner.

- further develop the necessary skills, experience and understanding required to observe, plan, deliver and review their practice across the EY curriculum.

- plan for and implement a holistic and anti-bias approach to children's play, learning and development.

- work collaboratively with parents (where appropriate) and have an understanding of working effectively in teams and with other professionals.

- meet and promote children's health, welfare and safety needs and the conditions that enable them to flourish.

For those who continue towards developing GPC, they will aim to gain experience of working with children up to the age of eight years old, develop skills of leading practice and demonstrate advocacy for children.

Choose below which task is more relevant for your working context.

Reflective task for practitioners in placement

Access the EYE criteria, or as appropriate, the GPC and read and familiarise yourself with the criteria or competencies.

- Highlight where you may already have gained experiences that will support you on your professional practice journey.

- Identify areas you will need to develop additional skills in or competencies.

This task may be completed over a few days, and it will support you to focus on what is relevant for you to succeed on your placement journey. Discuss your findings with your setting mentor, visiting tutor, a colleague or peer.

Reflective task for mentors

Access the EYE criteria, or as appropriate, the GPC and read and familiarise yourself with the criteria or competencies.

- Identify opportunities in the setting which may support students to gain experiences linked to the relevant criteria or competencies.

- Are there areas of practice which are not accessible to your mentee? If so, how may this be addressed?

Starting the placement experience

The safety and welfare of children is of utmost priority for all settings and anchored in the welfare requirements as set out by the EYFS Statutory Framework (DfE, 2021a). Therefore, everyone who comes into contact with children or vulnerable people, whether they are volunteering, in training or employed will need to demonstrate they are not barred from carrying out their role in the setting. An enhanced check via the Disclosure and Barring Service (DBS) therefore needs to be completed by all students, and only after receiving the certificate they will be able to attend their placement setting. This process is often completed via the training provider; for students in employment this will likely be carried out by the setting via their umbrella body (GOV.UK, 2022b).

It is important to develop and maintain professional relationships with all staff within the setting. You may ask, what does it mean to be professional? According to Creasy (2015), professionalism is shown in the dispositions students develop as part of their training for their future roles. This is mirrored in the benchmark statements for early childhood studies, which refer to the 'behaviours, attributes and competencies suited to early childhood professions at different levels, such as taking initiative, making things happen, reflecting, communicating, pivoting and adapting, taking responsibility, networking, developing personal effectiveness and managing risk taking' and refer to attributes such as open-mindedness, proactivity, curiosity, flexibility, self-efficacy and resilience amongst others (QAA, 2022, p7). For example, when receiving feedback, showing professionalism may mean reflecting on what was said and taking responsibility for actions in a self-reflective way.

Given the range of daily social interactions EY practitioners utilise as part of their everyday work commitments, they need to develop communication skills which support these interactions in a professional way. This is not only essential for early childhood care and education but also ensures a positive placement experience. Students will often need to adapt their communication style according to the situation: responding to emails from the visiting tutor, passing information relating to observations on to colleagues, and ensuring confidentiality at all times which require students to be well aware of and reflect on different ways of communicating and use appropriate communication styles.

Reflective task

- Reflect on the professional skills and attitudes outlined in the section above.

- As you prepare for your placement experience, define what being a professional means for you in the context of your early childhood education and care setting.

Role of the student

As part of developing students' professional practice, many training providers will share the expectations they have of students within the setting. Often this may take the form of a Code of Conduct for Professional Practice. As an exemplar of the professional expectations of students in placement in an early childhood setting, we have adapted the Code of Conduct used on the Early Childhood Studies course we are teaching on and hope this gives the reader valuable insights and a notion of what early childhood professionals should strive for. According to the Code of Practice we share with our students, it expected that students adhere to the professional expectations of the early childhood sector as part of their placement practice and demonstrate consistently high standards of personal and professional conduct.

Below outlined are some of the behaviours and attitudes that a Code of Conduct may include in order to maintain professional standards for conduct throughout a practitioner's career, and therefore public trust in the profession is maintained. These require student practitioners to uphold high standards of ethics and behaviour, within and outside the setting environment as they:

- treat children, families and staff with dignity, building relationships rooted in mutual respect, and whilst at all times observing proper boundaries appropriate to a practitioner's professional position.

- have regard for the need to safeguard children's well-being, in accordance with statutory provisions, policies and procedures.

- show tolerance of and respect for the rights of others.

- act according to values consistent with those promoted in the statutory documents regulating early childhood care and education, including democracy, the rule of law, individual liberty and mutual respect, and tolerance of those with different faiths and beliefs.

- are aware of their online profile, and mindful of how their interactions online can impact on their professional identity.

Further, as part of their placement experience practitioners should have professional regard for the ethos, policies and practices of the setting in which they are working and maintain high standards of attendance and punctuality. It is expected that practitioners have a good understanding of, and always act within, the statutory frameworks which set out their professional duties and responsibilities.

Induction to the setting

If you are not familiar with the location and area of your placement, it advisable to have researched the route to the placement setting and being aware of an alternative way to get there, should unforeseen circumstances require you to do so. This will ensure you arrive at your setting in plenty of time. If for any reason you arrive late or need to leave the setting early, this should be communicated promptly with the manager, mentor and, as appropriate, your training provider. If absence is unavoidable, follow the agreed training provider or settings' procedures. Usually, there is a great deal of information to take in on your first day in placement practice. You will be introduced to staff members, such as your mentor and the other staff members you will be usually working with. At the beginning of your placement practice, you should be introduced to Health and Safety procedures in the setting. You will need to know the important aspects of this, for example, what to do in case of a fire alarm, whether a planned fire drill is due, or in case of an unexpected fire alarm. In addition, you will be introduced to the setting's policies and procedures most relevant to you at this stage of your placement journey. In this respect you should find out if there are particular policies you need to become familiar with immediately or during the course of the placement. For example, should you be aware of the dress code required by the setting? What is seen as acceptable to wear may differ from setting to setting.

It is helpful to find out if students are expected to contribute to a fund for refreshments and if so, to whom they should make payments. You may enquire if there are rotas for washing up, or tidying staff rooms or other tasks related to housekeeping.

Demonstrating you are proactive and to get the most out of your placement we encourage you to find out if there are procedures for using consumable and non-consumable resources such as food items, craft materials and any restrictions you should be aware of. This may extend to how children's creative work is displayed in the setting.

Reflective task

As part of developing your professional practice, begin to get to know and reflect on the setting policies. Choose policies from the range of areas suggested: Health and Safety, Behaviour, Equal Opportunities, Child Protection or Safeguarding, Curriculum, Planning

- Check your understanding of the policies you have selected with a colleague, peer or your mentor.

- Reflect and note down how the policies you have chosen support your practice.

Engaging positively within the placement

The placement journey may start with the student practitioner observing routines and starting to interact and getting to know some of the children and staff within the setting. During the first few weeks students will be settling in and this will give them an opportunity to explore the key policies which will give a good grounding to their placement experience. Students will begin to work alongside staff and should be able to participate in setting up and clearing away. Observing an experienced practitioner leading story time or during a music or singing activity will prepare students to interact with and participate in the play of small groups of children both in and outside. The next step may be to find out about the setting's record keeping and planning; this will prepare the student practitioner for eventually planning and carrying out activities with a small group of children negotiated with their mentor and visiting tutor. All these tasks give the mentor opportunity to observe their mentee in practice and provide constructive feedback.

Challenges impacting on the placement experience

Students undertaking placement in settings may experience challenges which may be more severe than the usual difficulties associated with for instance managing time in placement or their academic studies. Student practitioners in many cases are juggling employment and university studies. This chapter will be supportive in addressing some of the barriers to the development of effective professional practice. Issues occurring may be personal, or related to academic studies, and should be responded to before they begin to significantly impact on the practice experience. In this context, it is important that the mentor has access to the details of the training provider and the relevant person to contact.

Reflective task

Student practitioner Myah is starting her placement this coming week at a day nursery setting, which has been allocated to her by the training provider.

- What would you suggest should be Myah's preparations before she starts her placement? Make a list in order of priority.

- How can her setting mentor ensure Myah's first week in the setting is supportive to her settling in and engaging positively with the opportunities in the setting?

Developing skills of reflection and the role of the reflective journal

Yates and Appleby (2014, p52) draw on the work of Reed and Cunning to consider reflective learning as 'one of the most valuable learning experiences we can undertake as it requires us to learn from our own experiences and actions'.

Placement practice offers student practitioners the necessary context that provides rich opportunities for reflective learning. Reflection should be a key aspect of EY practice as it supports the professional development of all practitioners and in this way is conducive to improved early childhood practice and provision. For example, student practitioners may reflect on how they meet the needs of individual children or reflect on issues relating to working in partnership with parents. They may think back on events and consider what went well and what did not and consider the reasons for this. Reflecting on practice can be challenging as it requires practitioners to examine their own values, beliefs and attitudes. Yates and Appleby (2014, p52) suggest 'true reflection involves the process of observing oneself and the behaviours, thoughts and feelings that are involved in an interaction or event and using those observations to inform future practice'. Keeping a reflective journal helps not only students in placement but also practitioners generally to capture experiences and events from practice they can reflect on and in this way develop their practice thoughtfully. You can find more details regarding the reflective journal in Chapter 9.

Reflective task

There are a number of theoretical models that are based on the notion of learning from experience and the reflective cycle (for example, Kolb, 1984).

- Carry out your own research on theoretical models that help you understand the value of reflection for your learning and professional development.

- Which model(s) do you consider as useful for your learning and development and note down why?

Whether students keep a digital or handwritten reflective journal, it is important that entries are made regularly, usually one entry for every day in practice. Students often struggle with beginning to write their reflective journal entries. It is not unusual for journal entries at the beginning of their placement journey to be more descriptive of happenings in the setting, rather than being reflective. With daily practice and gradual immersion in the reflective processes that may be happening in the placement setting, for example, during staff meetings, students will develop their journal writing skills. These will enable them to become more reflective. This could be supported through discussions with their mentor and visiting tutor. Being reflective means being curious and asking, why things may have happened the way they did and perhaps what could have been done differently. Being open to alternate possibilities that arise as a result of reflection will help to inform future practice. In this way reflective journal entries can capture the learning and development process of students in a meaningful way.

Reflective task

Read the extract of Myah's first reflective journal entry below which she wrote on her first day in placement and evaluate it in terms of its usefulness to support her learning and development in relation to her professional practice. Drawing on your learning from the previous task on researching models of reflection, how could she develop her reflective writing further?

> *[...]I was surprised that some of the children approached me to read a story to them as they had not met me before. At first, I did not know if I should follow the children's lead and became nervous as I wondered what my mentor and the staff in the room expected of me. As a result, I felt little uneasy when I sat with the group of children in the reading area. An approving nod from my mentor eased the situation and I found myself more relaxed and started reading [...]*

Assessment of practice

Preparing for a visit from the visiting tutor is crucial to making the visit a valuable learning experience that can propel learning and professional practice. The visiting tutor may want to see evidence of planning and implementation of activities. They will want to elicit feedback from the student and how they have engaged with the children, their mentor and colleagues. Where a planned activity has been carried out, visiting tutors want to see that any planning has been informed by observations of children and addresses their individual needs.

You may need to show an attendance time sheet that is up to date, so your assessor can ensure you are on track to meeting the required placement hours in the setting. Being able to discuss and show awareness of the assessment criteria, and how it links to professional practice will support students in planning and carrying out activities as well as guide interactions with children, colleagues and, where appropriate, parents.

Assessment visits are designed to observe students in an EY environment they should be familiar with and settled in. Visiting tutors are interested in the way students interact with children, families and staff in the setting, and these should be genuine and natural interactions. This will enable a more accurate assessment to be achieved. Often there is a specific time frame given for the observation of practice and the importance of planning for the visit is evident considering that many settings have fixed routines including specific activity times.

It is important to understand that the visits from the tutor are viewed as developmental, although you may receive a grade at the end of each visit. The assessment marks a point in time; however, when working with children and their families, learning and development of professional practice does not stop. There-fore, time should be made to reflect on the assessment and areas of strengths as well as areas for development should be identified as part of this process.

The advantage of the mentor being present in the setting is that they are able to observe the student on a regular basis and in their day-to-day interactions with the children, families and staff. This allows mentors to identify areas of strengths and development which may inform goals and target setting.

Reflective task

Imagine your tutor's visit is planned go ahead in two weeks from today. Prepare for your assessment visit by writing down all the things you need to consider, including the planning of the activity to be observed. Consider also the EYE qual-ification criteria or GPC, whichever is relevant to your context.

Develop your reflective skills by asking yourself the following question after you have carried out a planned activity in the setting:

1. What has gone well and what has not?

2. Which aspects of your practice need developing? (linked to the EYE qualifica-tion criteria or GPC)

3. What have you learnt so far by being with the children and experienced practitioners?

Summary

This chapter considered the aspect of assessed practice as a necessary part of early childhood practitioner's professional development. The historical contexts in which the student practitioner's practice is assessed have been discussed, so the reader gains insight into how these have been shaped over the previous two decades. We favoured a three-way model of assessed practice that ensures the perspectives of the placement student, their mentor and those of visiting tutors are each valued and contribute to students' professional development as part of their placement practice. This chapter outlined the aims of the placement experience for students and the importance of developing skills of reflection. We encouraged students to make effective use of a reflective journal to help them make meaning of their placement experience and learning. The skills developed will support students in understanding that reflective practice is a process that embraces life-long learning.

7 Assessment within the EYFS and KS1

Assessment plays an important part in helping parents, carers and practitioners to recognise children's progress, understand their needs, and to plan activities and support.

(DfE, 2021a, p18)

Why is knowledge and understanding of assessment important, and how can practitioners develop their practice in supporting assessments effectively?

This chapter introduces the reader to concepts of assessment within the Early Years Foundation Stage (EYFS) (DfE, 2021a) and the National Curriculum (NC) (DfE, 2013) in England with a focus on Key Stage 1 (KS1). It aims to introduce a range of assessments relevant to practice in the EYFS and KS1. This chapter will help you gain a better understanding of assessments. It will consider the impact legislation and policies have on the way assessments are carried out. Practitioners who have knowledge of a wide range of assessment practices can utilise these meaningfully, in order to support and promote a more child-centered approach. It discusses the statutory aspects of assessments as they feature in both the EYFS and KS1 and considers these in a way that supports students and practitioners in developing their practice in a critically reflective way. It offers guidance to help develop effective planning and introduces 'Documentation of Learning' as an alternative assessment.

CHAPTER OVERVIEW

In this chapter we aim to help you develop your understanding of:

- Assessment and the importance of assessment within the Early Years Foundation Stage (EYFS) and Key Stage 1 (KS1)

- Assessments in the EYFS and KS1 and their political context

- The different types of assessments in the EYFS and KS1

- The role of the practitioner in planning and carrying out assessments

- Assessment within different pedagogical and curricula contexts

---

You will find Chapters 2, 3, 4 and 8 link closely to the topics discussed within this chapter.

This chapter links to the relevant criteria for:

Early Years Educator (Department for Education and National College for Teaching and Leadership, 2019)

- 1.4 Analyse and explain how children's learning and development can be affected by their stage of development and individual circumstances.

- 1.7 Understand systematic synthetic phonics in the teaching of reading and a range of strategies for developing early literacy and mathematics.

- 1.9 Understand the current early education curriculum requirements.

- 3.1 Understand how to assess within the current early education curriculum framework using a range of assessment techniques.

- 3.2 Carry out and record observational assessment accurately.

- 3.3 Identify the needs, interests and stages of development of individual children.

- 3.4 Make use of formative and summative assessment, tracking children's progress to plan next steps and shape learning opportunities.

- 3.5 Discuss children's progress and plan the next stages in their learning with the key person, colleagues, parents and/or carers.

- 6.1 Work co-operatively with colleagues and other professionals to meet the needs of babies and children and enable them to progress.

- 6.2 Work in partnership with parents and/or carers to help them recognise and value the significant contributions they make to the child's health, well-being, learning and development.

- 6.3 Encourage parents and/or carers to take an active role in the child's play, learning and development.

Early Childhood Graduate Practitioner Competencies (Early Childhood Studies Degree Network, 2019)

- 1.2 Observe, support and extend young children's participation in their learning through following their needs and interests.

(Continued)

(Continued)

- 4.1 Know and understand the relevant early childhood curriculum frameworks and apply them in practice.

- 4.2 Apply a range of observation and research skills to co-construct young children's development, play and learning, encouraging independence and next steps.

- 6.3 Demonstrate an understanding of statutory guidance for children with special educational needs and disabilities (SEND) and protected characteristics.

- 6.4 Evidence skills in appropriate planning to address the care and early learning needs of individual young children with SEND and protected characteristics.

- 7.1 Evidence understanding of the importance of partnership with parents and/or caregivers in their role as infants and young children's first educators.

What is assessment in the Early Years Foundation Stage and Key Stage 1 and why is it important?

Assessment within Early Years settings is about collecting and evaluating information to help support the judgements and decisions we make about the children we work with. However, we must be cautious in the judgements and decisions that we make. The EYFS states that, 'when assessing whether an individual child is at the expected level of development, practitioners should draw on their knowledge of the child and their own expert professional judgement and should not be required to prove this through collection of physical evidence' (Department of Education (DfE), 2021a, p18). Remember that we assess children to help us be clear about what they know, what they have learnt, what they understand or what they are able to do. These assessments support and inform our planning for the children's individual needs in the short, medium and long term.

All state-funded schools in England must embed the NC programme of study for all children of statutory school age. Although many children start school earlier, the statutory school age refers to the term after the child has had their 5th birthday. The NC is structured into four key stages which relate to specific year groups and outlines what children should be taught within its 'core' and 'foundation subjects' (DfE, 2013, p6). At KS1 this relates to the attainment targets in the core subjects of English and Mathematics. The DfE (2014) demands the curriculum includes an assessment system that monitors children's learning and progress within subjects and which identifies whether children can be expected to meet the attainment targets at the end of each key stage. To help understand the assessment processes used in the Early Years and KS1 we will need to distinguish between formative and summative assessment processes and establish their purposes.

You will find that the term formative assessment is also referred to as assessment for learning. It aspires for children to develop a positive attitude towards learning and to be actively engaged in this process. Importantly, the learning intention of activities is made explicit to children, so there is an opportunity for them to self-direct their learning. It follows, rather than evaluating the outcome of a specific task or activity the focus is on children's engagement (Colwell, 2015). Assessment for learning requires practitioners to offer constructive feedback to children and to communicate this in a way that keeps children motivated, by focussing on their progress and achievement and by offering direction and different ways children can bring their learning forward (Hargreaves et al., 2018). Good practice will be child-centred and considerate of children's individual abilities, their understanding and development.

Summative assessment by contrast captures and evaluates children's knowledge and understanding at a specific point in time. These assessments typically take place at the beginning or endpoint of the academic year. Summative assessment measures children's achievement in relation to specific learning goals or attainment targets and within a given timeframe. It may not take account of individual children's circumstances which may have an impact on the assessment, and we discuss this in more detail further on in this chapter. As shown by Hargreaves (2018, p289) summative assessment may be referred to as 'assessment of learning', whereas formative assessment may be associated with 'assessment for learning'. However, both ways of assessing can support practitioners to plan for children's learning based on the evidence gained from children's current achievement. Summative assessments carried out at the beginning of the academic year, such as the Reception Baseline Assessment (RBA) give practitioners opportunity to plan for a differentiated curriculum that offers potential for all children to make progress.

What is the Early Years Foundation Stage and what is the relationship between the political context and assessments?

For those of you who may not be familiar with the EYFS (DfE, 2021a), it is a statutory curriculum or set of minimum standards that supports the learning, development and care of children from birth to 5 years old. It was implemented by then Department for Children, Schools and Families (now Department for Education) in September 2008 and has been updated, revised and amended several times. It continues to be a controversial policy as many believe that it is not appropriate to have such a curriculum for very young children and debates continue (Palaiologou, 2021). However, it is important to note that the EYFS was introduced through legislation, the Childcare Act 2006, and is a legal requirement for all settings in England caring for children from 0 to 5 years and therefore not a choice whether to implement or not. As mentioned 'the EYFS has been amended several times with revisions such as changes to Early Learning Goals and greater emphasis on safety and school readiness' (Palaiologou, 2021, pxiii). The EYFS was influenced by research such as the Effective Provision of Pre-School Education Project also known as EPPE which showed the benefits of high-quality provision on children's learning and development (Sylva et al., 2004).

What is the purpose of the EYFS?

'The EYFS seeks to provide:

- quality and consistency in all Early Years settings, so that every child makes good progress and no child gets left behind
- a secure foundation through planning for the learning and development of each individual child, and assessing and reviewing what they have learned regularly
- partnership working between practitioners and with parents and/or carers
- equality of opportunity and anti-discriminatory practice, ensuring that every child is included and supported'.

(Department for Education, 2021a, p5)

The EYFS has four guiding principles that as practitioners you should use in shaping practice within Early Years settings. These are:

1. Every child is a unique child, who is constantly learning and can be resilient, capable, confident and self-assured

2. Children learn to be strong and independent through positive relationships

3. Children learn and develop well in enabling environments with teaching and support from adults, who respond to their individual interests and needs and help them to build their learning over time. Children benefit from a strong partnership between practitioners and parents or carers

4. The importance of learning and development: Children develop and learn at different rates. The framework covers the education and care of all children in Early Years provision, including children with SEND

(Department for Education, 2021a)

There is a strongly held view that in order to meet relevant external outcomes, such as those set by the Office for Standards in Education (Ofsted) or the local government, carrying out assessments has become crucial in both the EYFS and KS1. We therefore see continuous assessments and evaluation throughout these key stages (Rawding, 2019). In section two of the EYFS (DfE, 2021a, p18), for example, it is highlighted that, 'ongoing assessment (also known as formative assessment) is an integral part of the learning and development process' of children. It is an expectation from government and Ofsted that regular observations and evaluations of children's learning and development are shared with parents ensuring that they are kept up to date with their children's progress. In this context, see our discussions in Chapter 3 'Working with Diverse Families and a Range of Professionals'.

Assessment within the NC is evident through summative assessments such as national tests at the end of KS1, when children are in Year 1 and Year 2 and usually between 6 and 7 years old. Children will start KS2 in Year 3, when they are between 7 and 8 years old. At the end of KS2, children will again take part in national assessments. These occur towards the end of Year 6, when children are between 10 and 11 years old. National assessments provide useful information on children's achievements overall and may also identify any national trends. For example, those observed during the COVID-19 pandemic included falling attainment levels which then impacted on young children's learning and development (DfE, 2021b). A limitation of national assessments is that they are only a snapshot of achievement captured within a narrow timeframe and therefore does not always offer a full picture of a child's achievements. We have to be mindful that the focus of national assessments is not always on the achievements of individual children. In some circumstances, the attention is on the school's achievement and their place in the national league tables. As Hargreaves et al. (2018, p290) point out, the numerical data provided may be used to 'make schools accountable by allowing comparisons of achievement across schools'.

Reflective task

Download and read the section on assessment in the EYFS statutory framework document. What is your understanding of 'ongoing assessment' as outlined in the document (DfE, 2021a, p18)?

- What does 'ongoing assessment' look like in your setting?

- Reflect on how 'ongoing assessment' enables practitioners to support children's learning and development.

- Can you think of ways to enhance and develop aspects of 'ongoing assessment' in your setting?

- Make notes in your reflective journal.

Now access the current KS1 teacher assessment guidance published online. At the time of the writing this book, this can be accessed via the Standards & Testing Agency (2022).

- What does 'day-to-day formative assessment' look like in a KS1 setting?

- Reflect on how 'day-to-day formative assessment' enables practitioners to support children's learning and development?

Setting policies and assessments

Legislation and setting policies are closely linked to how we implement assessments, and you will recall in Chapter 2 we discussed legislation and its impact on policy. In order to ensure that the EYFS (DfE, 2021a) is implemented in line with the Childcare Act 2006. Settings generally include assessment within their policy portfolio. This may contain the following:

- the rationale for the policy which clarifies that it has been developed in conjunction with Department for Education (DfE) guidance, legislation and works in tandem with other setting policies such as the equal opportunities and the SEND policy,

- clarification of the intent of the policy ensuring that every child is able to learn and develop well,

- an outline of the setting's responsibility to ensure that all staff are aware, understand and know how to implement the policy,

- identifying any areas of concern relating to children's development or emotional needs,

- continuous formative and summative assessments which helps staff and parents understand how the child makes progress and is performing in line with national and local expectations (for example, the EYFS).

- at the end of the EYFS a profile is completed which gives a holistic picture of the child's knowledge, understanding and abilities. It enables the setting to understand where the child is in relation to the Early Learning Goals and how ready they are for Year 1.

- how, throughout the child's attendance at the setting, evidence will be collected to support judgements of the child's progress. These may include written or drawn evidence, observations, photographic evidence, video, audio or electronic recordings, information from parents, other professionals and where appropriate the child.

Reflective task

Find out whether your setting has an assessment policy. It may be that a different name is used.

- What does the policy say about assessing children?

- Is there anything within the policy that you do not understand? If yes, what is it that you are not clear about? Share your query with another colleague, student, mentor or tutor.

- How may observations (planned and unplanned) inform the assessment of a child?

What are the different types of assessment outlined in the EYFS and what can be learned from observing children?

Observations made by practitioners within the setting and those shared with staff by parents that take place outside of the setting environment both help to support effective formative assessments. Practitioners who are knowledgeable about children's interests and achievements can effectively plan for each child's learning and development in partnership with parents. Guidance documentation such as 'Development Matters' on supporting children's learning and development within the EYFS from the DfE (2021c) and 'Birth to 5 Matters' (Early Education, 2021) clearly highlight that practitioners' time should be dedicated to the children they care for rather than completing unnecessary paperwork. This means, whilst it important to observe children, this should not unduly take time away from practitioners spending valuable time with children. Early Education (2021, p38) advocates practitioners should observe children 'as a part of all activity', emphasising observations are 'most often held in the mind of the practitioner but may sometimes be documented' so practitioners can plan for their own next steps in supporting and extending children's learning. For students and practitioners, who are developing their skills to record observations, capturing what they have seen and heard in a notebook or on post-it notes can be an effective way to develop proficiency and confidence in how to observe children and then to record these observations. In addition, it will give students in placement practice valuable insight into how children learn and develop, and it helps to identify children's interests, their likes, dislikes and abilities (McMahon and Watson, 2019).

Reflective task

- What is the role of observations in your setting in relation to assessment?

- Give an example how observations are used to inform planning and formative assessments in the setting.

- What are potential challenges when observing children across the age range which applies to EYFS (0–5 years old)?

- Reflect and note down why it is important to share observations with parents (Chapter 3 will offer helpful prompts).

The EYFS (DfE, 2021a) stipulates the following assessments as essential:

The progress check at the age of two years is an assessment where the practitioners have the responsibility to review the child's progress and write a summary of their development within the prime areas of learning and development. The prime areas are 'communication and language, physical development and personal, social and emotional development' (DfE, 2021a, p8). The child's strength in these areas and those that are 'less than expected' must be identified in the summary or report (DfE, 2021a, p18). It is important to note that parents must always be involved in the process. Where there are major concerns in relation to a child's learning or development, these must be targeted, planned for, and supported. As discussed in Chapter 3 on working with diverse families and other professionals, parents must be informed and involved and where necessary include others such as the Special Educational Needs Coordinator (SENCO) or specific health professionals.

One of the challenges highlighted by Howard and Hutchinson (2021, p155) of the progress check is that 'the quality of the report can vary from extremely detailed, which means it is time consuming to create, to something that is barely more than a few words and gives very little insight in terms of understanding the individual and their achievements or their needs, yet both meet the statutory requirements'.

Reflective task

- If you are a student or practitioner in a setting attended by children aged 2 years old, find out how the progress check is implemented.

- Reflect on the process, engagement with parents, the child's experience and the final report.

- In your reflective journal, note down the strengths and limitations of the progress check at age 2.

- How do you believe this process could be improved?

- Discuss your findings with your colleague, mentor or tutor.

The beginning of the Reception year is another point at which the child is assessed; this is known as the reception baseline assessment (RBA). This assessment is usually carried out within the first six weeks of the child entering Reception class and came into force in September 2021. The assessments are carried out through a range of different activities and practical tasks focussing on language, communication, and literacy (LCL) and mathematics.

The final assessment within the EYFS is the Early Years Foundation Stage Profile (EYFSP) (DfE, 2022c). This assessment is carried out at the end of the EYFS and is to be carried out no later than 30th of June in that term for every child. The EYFSP is also a statutory requirement and must be completed by the following establishments/organisations:

1. Local authority-maintained schools

2. Non-maintained independent schools

3. Academies and free schools

4. Nurseries
5. Private nursery schools
6. Pre-schools/playgroups
7. Childminding.

(Howard and Hutchinson, 2021, 156)

As with the two-year progress check it is important that practitioners use their 'own knowledge and professional judgement of a child to inform discussions with parents and carers, and any other adults whom the teacher, parent or carer judges can offer a useful contribution' (DfE, 2021a, p19).

The role of the practitioner or key person in assessment

The practitioner or key person will play a vital role in the assessment of the child. They are in a unique position to provide a holistic and rich picture of the child. Including the voices of parents and other relevant professionals in the assessment will help create a more balanced and objective view, rather than a subjective perspective of the child's learning and development. You will find additional information on the role of practitioners in Chapter 3 on Working with Diverse Families and a Range of Professionals and Chapter 4 on Leading Practice. Ensuring an anti-bias approach is essential when documenting the child's progress. This approach should be supported within the settings' equality policy and is discussed in more detail within Chapter 8 on Inclusive Practice. What is written down on paper formally can and will impact on the views, judgements and decisions that are made about the child, particularly if the child has a special educational need. This view is supported by others such as Howard and Hutchinson (2021, p169) who suggest that 'valuable information and engagement with parents, carers and others including specialists such as health visitors, educational psychologists and social workers, is the collaborative assessment process that helps with the early identification of additional needs'.

It is important to be mindful when assessing children and to take into consideration any factors or particular circumstances that could obscure your judgements. For example, if the child is new to the setting and is still settling in, or if there are any issues at home such as a recent break-up of parents, illness, bereavement or a new sibling in the family.

The role of the student practitioner is key in supporting the assessment process. You may be called upon to assist in carrying out and record observations or support the planning and implementation of activities for a practical assessment. However, this will of course depend on your abilities, growing experience, knowledge and understanding of the assessment processes overall. Reflective practice can support you in developing your skills, knowledge and understanding of the assessment process. Keeping a reflective learning journal helps you assess more clearly what you are seeing, hearing, feeling and learning. By keeping a reflective journal your experiences 'can be unpicked and debated, internally and with peers, to help the development of greater awareness, the increase in abilities and skills, and can begin to form the basis of your own theoretical development' (Leeson, 2019, p396).

Reflective task

- Observe a child engaged in an activity within the setting on one of the prime areas of learning for example: communication and language, personal, social and emotional developed, physical development.

- Record in your reflective journal what you see and hear.

- From that observation, evaluate and assess the child's learning and development drawing on your knowledge of the EYFS and its guidance documentation (see DfE, 2021b; Early Education, 2021).

- Reflect on how you can support the child in this area of learning.

- Discuss your evaluation and assessment with your mentor or tutor.

What are the different types of assessment in Key Stage 1?

There are three types of assessment which dominate KS1 practice. First and foremost, these include 'day-to-day formative assessments' which are carried out to inform teaching on an ongoing basis (Standards & Testing Agency, 2022). They are undertaken by practitioners on a daily basis and can draw on a range of evidence such as marked work in children's workbooks, questions and answers during class, or observational assessment (McIntosh, 2015). The way these formative assessments are carried out should be guided by the school's assessment policy.

Secondly, in-school summative assessment should enable practitioners understand how well children have performed at the end of a particular teaching period. According to McIntosh (2015) they should be implemented in a meaningful way and not add unnecessarily to practitioners' workload. Practitioners in a KS1 classroom are expected to make assessments of pupils in Mathematics, Science and English reading and writing (Standards & Testing Agency, 2022). McIntosh (2015) recommends it should be implemented in line with the school policy and in implementing these, schools are encouraged to develop their own assessment systems. Assessments carried out by practitioners in the core subjects are shared with parents individually, and parents can expect to receive a report for their child at the end of KS1 and KS2.

Finally, the statutory summative assessments within KS1 include the phonics screening check at the end of Year 1. This check applies to children who will reach the age of six by the end of Year 1 and who are attending a maintained school setting, an academy or a free school. In addition, at the end of KS1, children will be assessed in English reading and Mathematics through 'teacher assessment' (TA) as required by the Standards & Testing Agency (2021, p34). These assessments enable the government to understand how children perform across England in line with NC assessment standards.

Assessment within KS1 is strengthened through both internal and external moderation processes. Moderation ensures that assessment meets a standard consistent with national expectations and ensures it is a fair, effective and as far as possible an unbiased process. It is carried out by the local authority (LA), who is required to moderate each school within their LA at least every four years (Standards & Testing Agency, 2021). In this way the government ensures schools as well as teachers are accountable, should children's attainment fall below expected levels (Colwell, 2015). Where such shortfalls are visible within specific geographic areas, this may, for instance, indicate a need for specific training of staff within schools or highlight a need for more support staff, for example. To ensure all children can demonstrate their knowledge and understanding in ways most appropriate to their talents, Hargreaves et al. (2018) suggest a wide range of assessment methods should be used when children are assessed. In this way children are enabled to demonstrate their knowledge, skills and abilities drawing on their individual strengths. The Standards & Testing Agency (2021, p35) requires TA to be differentiated and presented as 'pupil can' statements which show if children are

- working towards the expected standard
- working at the expected standard
- working at greater depth.

The NC promotes the idea of assessments being inclusive, with teachers 'setting high expectations for every pupil [...] and using appropriate assessment to set targets which are deliberately ambitious' (DfE, 2013, p8). Children who at the end of KS1 are working below the standard of NC assessment but are engaged in subject-specific study will be assessed using the pre-key stage standards. These standards differentiate between four levels and are based on judgements by the practitioner. It is expected the assessment is made from a wide range of evidence gathered through children's engagement with the daily learning opportunities and activities offered in the setting and which relate to the subjects of English and Mathematics (Standards & Teaching Agency, 2020a).

Children who are not engaged in subject-specific study due to having a 'serious cognitive impairments and learning difficulties, which lead to significant delays in reaching developmental milestones' will be assessed using the engagement model (Standards & Teaching Agency, 2020b, p7). Effective assessment using the engagement model relies on practitioners' skills of observation and reflection, as well as partnership working with parents and professionals to support their assessment of the child in five areas of engagement: exploration, realisation, anticipation, persistence and initiation (Standards & Teaching Agency, 2020b).

Within the NC it is expected that, for example, 'a good assessment policy in schools recognises that both assessment objectives and assessment outcomes can be shared with parents to help them support their children's learning' (McIntosh, 2015, p28). Further, when decisions are made whether a child should be participating in statutory assessments, for example, due to special educational needs, parents must be informed (Standards & Testing Agency, 2021). In contrast to the strong underpinning value of parent partnership within the EYFS (DfE, 2021a), the head teacher is able to make decisions on, for example, the participation of pupils in statutory assessments relating to the relevant key stages of the NC. Although parents must be informed of such a decision, and have a right of appeal, it is far from the spirit of partnership working usually experienced by parents within the EYFS (DfE, 2021a).

Assessment within a range of pedagogical and curricula approaches

Having gained insight into assessment in the context of the EYFS and KS1, it is important to point out that 'what' is assessed, 'how' and 'why' it is assessed not only relies on the political and geographical context but is also influenced and specific to pedagogical approaches and their curricula. Where curriculum frameworks are implemented in early childhood care and education, these are each underpinned by distinct values and principles and the way the child is viewed. For example, the impact of the four EYFS (DfE, 2021a) guiding principles of the unique child, positive relationships, enabling environments with teaching and support from adults and the importance of learning and development are visible in the way assessments are realised in early childhood practice. Each child is valued as an individual, and practitioners observe children's interests and plan according to their individual needs. This process includes usually the key person building relationships with each child and with their parents and, where indicated, through cooperation and partnership working with other professionals. This then provides the foundation for a curriculum that meets the learning and development needs of each child, and a clear role for the practitioner in supporting children's learning 'to ensure they are ready for year 1' (DfE, 2021a, p7).

We argue, developing professional practice should include openness and awareness of alternate ways the curriculum and role of the adult can be realised in early childhood settings. Being able to draw on a wide range of perspectives on assessment, for example, helps practitioners to reflect on and develop their own practice in an informed way. Much can be learned from practice outside England. You may be aware of pedagogical approaches that value documentation of learning as a way of making children's learning and development visible. This happens, for example in the early childhood settings of Reggio Emilia in Italy, where values such as community, respectful interactions and co-construction of learning are underpinning pedagogical practice. Documentation of learning is at the core of the Mosaic approach (Clark, 2017) and the New Zealand Curriculum Te Whariki (Ministry of Education, 2017). Clark and Moss (2011) have been inspired by Reggio Emilia early childhood settings, which is visible in the values expressed in the title of their book: Listening to Young Children: The Mosaic approach. Within the curriculum Te Whariki the principles of empowerment, holistic development, family and community and relationships also underpin the assessment process visible in the portfolios of children's learning and are enriched through narrative form of documentation: learning stories, influenced by the work of Margaret Carr (Ministry of Education, 2017).

Reflective task

Research the

- Mosaic approach
- Reggio Emilia approach
- Te Whariki curriculum in New Zealand
- Use Table 7.1 to note down your findings

	How are children assessed?	What is the role of the practitioner in assessment?	Underpinning values and principles	Consideration of children's rights (Unicef, 1989)?
National Curriculum (KS1) (DfE, 2013)				
Mosaic approach				
Reggio Emilia				
Te Whariki (Ministry of Education, 2017)				
EYFS (DfE, 2021a)				
Can you think of other approaches?				

Table 7.1   Researching approaches to pedagogy and curriculum

(Continued)

(Continued)

We have left additional boxes for you to research curriculum and pedagogical approaches that relate to areas you would like to research across the globe.

- Reflect on your findings and how these relate to what you have learnt about assessment in the EYFS.

- Is there anything you would like to see put into practice or changed within the EYFS?

- Reflect on how assessment practice you have come across values children as rights holders. You may find reading Chapter 1 helpful with this task.

Summary

This chapter has aimed to demonstrate the importance of assessment for practitioners who are working within the EYFS or KS1 settings. You will have developed an understanding of both formative and summative assessments within both these stages and how these may be implemented in settings in England. The introduction of the NC and the EYFS led to national standards being set for practice in early childhood education and care and in the key stages that follow. The chapter shows that the political context impacts on the 'what', 'how' and 'why' of assessment practice in early childhood and in school settings. You have been introduced to the role the practitioner plays as part of assessing children within the EYFS and KS1 and this includes working in partnership with parents. We have included reflective tasks throughout the chapter in order to support you in making links to your own practice and working context. Lastly, we took a look at assessment within a range of pedagogical and curriculum approaches to encourage you to scrutinise selected approaches in order to gain a deeper, more global understanding of assessment practice.

8 Inclusive practice

*Children should be treated fairly regardless of race, religion or abilities.
This applies no matter what they think or say; what type of family they
come from; what language(s) they speak; what their parents do; whether
they are girls or boys; whether they have a disability or whether they are
rich or poor.*

(DCSF, 2008)

Why is knowledge and understanding of inclusive practice important for all practitioners and professionals and what might effective practice look like?

This chapter aims to promote an inclusive approach to Early Years (EY) practice founded on the values and principles of education for social justice (ESJ). Using case studies, together with integration of the current policy context will show how an inclusive approach can be realised in EY settings. It will demonstrate how students and practitioners within EY settings can support inclusive practice. Consideration of the challenges that may present themselves will also be addressed.

CHAPTER OVERVIEW

In this chapter we will consider:

- What is inclusion and why is it important?

- What the values and principles of anti-discriminatory and anti-bias practice are

- What is ESJ and how can it be supported within settings?

- What is inclusive practice?

- How can we support inclusive practice and positive interactions with children, families and colleagues?

- The challenges and barriers to inclusion and inclusive practice.

You will find that Chapters 1, 2, 3, 4 and 7 link closely to the topics discussed within this chapter.

This chapter links to the relevant criteria for:

Early Years Educator (Department for Education and National College for Teaching and Leadership, 2019)

- 2.2 Ensure plans fully reflect the stage of development, individual needs and circumstances of children.

- 2.8 Model and promote positive behaviours expected of children.

- 2.9 Support children to manage their own behaviour in relation to others.

- 2.10 Understand when a child is in need of additional support.

- 2.11 Plan and provide activities to meet additional needs, working in partnership with parents and/or carers and other professionals, where appropriate.

- 6.2 Work in partnership with parents and/or carers to help them recognise and value the significant contributions they make to the child's health, well-being, learning and development.

Early Childhood Graduate Practitioner Competencies (Early Childhood Studies Degree Network, 2019).

- 1.2 Evidence knowledge, understanding and application in practice of pedagogy that supports inclusion.

- 1.3 Know how to identify infants and young children who may require additional support and how to refer to appropriate services.

- 6.1 Evidence knowledge, understanding and application in practice of pedagogy that supports inclusion.

- 6.2 Know how to identify infants and young children who may require additional support and how to refer to appropriate services.

- 6.3 Demonstrate an understanding of statutory guidance for children with Special Educational Needs and Disabilities and Protected Characteristics.

- 6.4 Evidence skills in appropriate planning to address the care and early learning needs of individual young children with special educational needs and/or disabilities and Protected Characteristics.

This chapter explores the importance of inclusion and inclusive practice within early childhood. It considers legislation, policies and the impact they can have on children, families and staff. Relevant definitions will be discussed to support your knowledge and understanding in areas of inequality. It also looks at some of challenges and barriers that hinder inclusion and considers how these could be overcome. The chapter requires a great deal of self-reflection, awareness and understanding of your own attitudes and biases relating to issues of inequality. It will need you to challenge your knowledge and understanding of inclusive practice in the hope that you will be fully onboard with anti-discriminatory practice and what that entails.

What is inclusion and why is it important?

There are numerous definitions to explain what inclusion is. The Early Childhood Forum (2022, p1) states that 'inclusion is a process of identifying, understanding and breaking down the barriers to participation and belonging'. You may think why is this statement important?

Inclusion is important wherever we are, as it makes us feel as though we belong and comfortable in the spaces that we navigate. Whether we are at work, at home or out with friends we all want to feel we are accepted and valued for who we are and not to be discriminated against due to what we look like, our beliefs or our sexual orientation. Therefore, we all have an obligation as part of society to ensure we are inclusive to everyone. Working within settings we come into contact with parents, children, staff, professionals and a whole range of other stakeholders. When working with the public or within a public setting we are obligated and have a responsibility to encourage and support inclusive practice. Inclusion is the bedrock of good practice and must be underpinned and embedded in our day-to-day work.

Key definitions for this chapter

Below are some useful definitions that will help you understand some of the discussion that may be referred to within this chapter or more generally in conversations in settings or within relevant readings.

What is a stereotype?

Having a fixed and firm idea or an over-simplified generalised understanding of a person or group of people. For example, all Jamaican families eat rice and peas and chicken on a Sunday.

What is prejudice?

Having a negative opinion or attitude of someone or a group of people based on ignorance or incorrect information. For example, you may believe that people with a physical disability should not work with children. Prejudice can also lead to discriminatory actions such as being racist or sexist. These terms will be explained further on in the chapter.

What is discrimination?

Discrimination is when someone or a group of people are being treated unfairly. It includes the systematic and institutionalised mistreatments of certain groups by the dominant society in order to deny them equal access to resources or services. Unlike with prejudice which involves negative thoughts (opinions), discrimination is a purposeful behaviour and is an action and something that impacts on others. For example, Mark was not employed as a baby room leader, as he is a man. You may rightly see this judgement is a result of being prejudice, for example believing that men are not suited to work with very young children. This is a form of direct discrimination under the Equality Act 2010 as someone's sex is the one of the protected characteristics.

Indirect discrimination

Indirect discrimination may involve policies, practices and services that could disadvantage someone who falls within any of the protected characteristics. For example, if you have a parent who has a physical disability and uses a wheelchair, and the setting does not have ramps or an appropriate way for that parent to access the building easily this could put them at a disadvantage. Where possible, adjustments need to be made to enable the parent to access the building.

It is against the Equality Act 2010 to discriminate against anyone because of:

1. Age

2. Gender reassignment

3. Being married or in a civil partnership

4. Being pregnant or on maternity leave

5. Having a disability

6. Your race including colour, nationality, ethnic or national origin

7. Religion or belief

8. Sex

9. Sexual orientation

These are called 'Protected Characteristics' and you are protected from discrimination:

- At work

- In education

- As a consumer

- When using public services

- When buying or renting property

- As a member or guest of a private club or association.

What is racism?

Racism is discriminatory behaviour and the Equality Act 2010 includes race as a protected characteristic. Therefore any instances where racism is suspected or occurs can be legally challenged and brought to court. An example of racism would be denying someone employment due to their skin colour or religious belief. Lane (2008, p31) defines racism as 'all those practices and procedures that both historically and in the present, disadvantage and discriminate against people because of their skin colour, ethnicity, culture, religion, nationality or language'.

What is sexism?

Sexism as a form of direct discrimination which occurs when a person is treated less favourably due to their sex or gender. For example, if you are breastfeeding in a public place and you are being asked to stop feeding your baby. Under the Equality Act 2010 'it is unlawful to discriminate against a woman because she is breast-feeding. This means that you need to allow women to whom you are providing goods, facilities, or services to breastfeed if they so wish' (Government Equalities Office, 2010, p10).

What do we mean by culture?

Culture is best defined as a way of life, how particular groups of people or individuals in society live, what they eat, drink, wear the festivals they celebrate and the beliefs they have. Culture also includes the values they have, and attitudes to the way they raise their children. The roles and responsibilities within the family, their relationships, behaviours and ways of doing things that are often passed down through generations. We must be mindful that cultures may evolve and change over time.

What do we mean by diversity?

Diversity is about honouring and valuing difference and uniqueness. A diverse society includes individuals and groups from different cultures, religions, socio-economic backgrounds, those with different life experiences, opinions, perspectives, abilities and age. Within the context of this book diversity describes the full range of differences that exist between young children and their families in the setting.

Reflective task

If you feel comfortable and safe, speak with a colleague, tutor, friend or partner. Can you identify a time when you or someone you know may have been discriminated against or disadvantaged?

- How did you (or they) feel?

(Continued)

(Continued)

- What did you do or what action if any did you take as a result of this experience?
- How may this experience have impacted on you (or someone you know)?
- How would you respond if put in a similar situation again?

What do we mean by equal opportunities?

Equal opportunities are about levelling the playing field to enable everyone to have an equal and fair chance. It is *not* about treating everyone the same. If we treated everyone the same, we could easily discriminate unintentionally against them. For example, in relation to disabilities, it is important to be aware that there are different forms of disability, such as those that require the use of a wheelchair. However, there are disabilities such as mental health conditions including depression or autism which may often be hidden and not always visible. Equal opportunities means having the same opportunities in life as others and this could involve being given more support if needed. The term is often loosely associated with issues around employment and access to services, and allowing everyone the opportunity to compete for jobs. For example, job adverts may mention applications from BAME (Black, Asian Minority Ethnic) groups are welcome as these groups are often underrepresented in some occupations, for instance the police (UK Parliament, 2021).

What do we mean by equality?

The Equality and Human Rights Commission (2018) suggests that equality is about enabling individuals to have equal opportunities, rights or status to become included in society. Dickins (2014) considers that equality is the result of putting the process of inclusion fully into practice. Fundamentally it consists of equality of access, equality of opportunity and anti-discriminatory practices, policies, and procedures that support inclusive practice.

What then do we mean by equity?

Equity is linked to fairness and social justice. It is about recognising that some of us and specific groups of people are more privileged and get a head start. We do not all begin from the same start line and therefore will need adjustments to support us and rebalance the inequality and disadvantage that some of us face. If you have a learning difficulty such as dyslexia, a physical disability or are living in poverty, this may disadvantage you. Equity is about putting processes in place to ensure disadvantage is not a barrier to opportunities.

What do we mean by social justice?

If you are unfamiliar with the term social justice, it is about the fair distribution of opportunities within society. It links to equality and aspires to enable all to be able to access resources, services and participate in society which is important to all of us.

What do we mean by inequality?

Inequality involves not being considered or treated equally. Many minority groups as discussed above may fall within the BAME group and often do not get similar opportunities to access services and resources. Inequality often occurs when there are clear boundaries in society that prevent people from attaining equal status despite their hard work and effort towards attaining specific goals. Groups and individuals may also experience inequality in terms of access to education, health and nutrition, security, power, social inclusion, income and assets.

What do we mean by ethnicity?

When we speak of someone's ethnicity, it is often linked to their physical traits. It also refers to an individual's identification with a group sharing some or all of the same culture, lifestyle, language, religion and history.

Reflective task

Consider the following questions which you can adapt to your context, reflect on them and try to answer honestly.

- Does the setting encourage and celebrate every child's uniqueness? If yes, how? If not, why not and how could this be developed?

- Does the setting treat children and families equally and with respect? If yes, how? If not, why not and how could this be developed?

- Does the setting include and support each child regardless of their cultural and linguistic background, gender, socio-economic circumstances or disability? If yes, how? If not, why not and how could this be developed?

- Do the resources provided ensure that every child is able to participate in activities/ curriculum? If yes, how? If not, why not and how could this be developed?

- If you had to score the effectiveness of inclusive practice, what score would you rate the setting and why? Out of a range from 0 – 10: 0 would suggest poor and 10 as being excellent.

Supporting inclusive practice

In order for all settings to support the Equality Act 2010 and ensure that they are not discriminating against anyone, equality policies are required to be put in place and adhered to. It forms part of the EY Ofsted inspection to ensure that settings are meeting their obligations under the Equality Act 2010 and the Education and Skills Act 2008 (Ofsted, 2019b).

Many of you will have heard or seen the acronym SEND or reference made to the SEND code of practice (Department for Education (DfE) and Department of Health (DoH), 2015). What does it mean and why is it relevant? The SEND (Special Educational Needs and Disability) code of practice 0–25 gives statutory guidance to all involved in the care and education of children and young people who may or have SEND. The Code of Practice links to the Children and Families Act 2014 (discussed in Chapter 2) and should be followed by all settings and local authorities who have responsibility to support children and young people. Children who have SEND are considered children in need under the Children Act 1989.

The definition of a child in need according to the Section 17 of the Children Act 1989 is if they are unlikely to achieve or maintain or have the opportunity of achieving, or maintaining, a reasonable standard of health or development without the provision of services by a Local Authority. This also applies if their health or development is likely to be significantly or further impaired, without the provision of such services or if they are disabled. Settings must therefore have a clear SEND policy in place, and this helps in the promotion of inclusion, and it is important that policies use appropriate and positive language when referring to children with SEND.

Reflective task

Download and read the SEND code of practice: 0–25 years statutory guidance for organisations which work with and support children and young people who have SEND (DfE and DoH, 2015) and answer the following questions.

- When did the SEND code of practice come into force?

- Who is considered as having SEND?

- Take a look at your settings' SEND policy and consider how effective it is. When we say effective, we mean how well it works or delivers for the children, families and staff. Are children with SEND fully included and have access to the full curriculum?

- What have you learnt about the settings' responsibilities towards their work with children who may have SEND?

- Why is it important to work in partnership with children and families?

The role of the SENCO (Special Educational Needs Co-ordinator)

Settings by law must have a designated person in the role as SENCO to ensure that children with SEND are supported effectively. The SENCO must be qualified or have relevant experience and training for the role which we discussed in detail within Chapter 4. The EYFS (DfE, 2021a) makes it a requirement that all EY settings make arrangements and identify a suitable person for the role. It is important to note that childminders also have this responsibility.

The code of practice (DfE and DoH, 2015, p89) states the following:

The role of the SENCO involves:

1. Ensuring all practitioners in the setting understand their responsibilities to children with SEN and the setting's approach to identifying and meeting SEN,

2. Advising and supporting colleagues,

3. Ensuring parents are closely involved throughout and that their insights inform action taken by the setting and

4. Liaising with professionals or agencies beyond the setting.

Inclusive practice

As discussed in Chapter 1, article 2 of the UNCRC (Unicef, 1989) refers to non-discrimination of children and article 3 refers to always considering the best interest of the child in all decisions being made or actions taken that affect them. Dickins (2014) highlights the foundations of inclusive practice and discusses basic attitudes to inclusive practice recognising that:

1. Each child is a unique and valuable individual

2. We should support positive approaches to behaviour management

3. We should have a can-do approach to children's achievements

4. We should be respectful and use positive language

5. Positive and collaborative relationships with parents and carers are crucial

6. There should be strong and committed leadership and management.

Inclusive practice is not just concerned with children who may have a SEND it is also concerned with having inclusive values, an ethos and a culture that supports all forms of inclusion (Nutbrown et al., 2013). Whalley (2008) links this to principles that guide practice and policies. This should include consideration of the environment, accessibility, the curriculum, parental involvement, training and development, particular roles, and responsibilities, for example, those of the SENCO and key persons.

Challenging inequalities

It is important that as a staff team you can challenge any form of inequality. Creating a setting where staff can feel empowered and safe to raise concerns, issues and question practice is essential to supporting inclusive practice. This could be through in-house training, team meetings (informal) or through tailored training (formal) for the team as a whole. Continuous reflection and evaluation of practice is key to supporting change and inclusion. Settings need to:

- Be proactive in addressing any barriers to inclusion

- Ensure policies and procedures are regularly reviewed (yearly would be ideal) around inclusion

- Continually develop a positive attitude. When we refer to a positive attitude, we mean focussing on what we can do to improve things or situations rather than having a negative or defeatist attitude

- Encourage an anti-discriminatory approach.

What is anti-discriminatory practice?

As highlighted by Dickins (2014), anti-discriminatory practice, which many of you may also refer to as anti-bias practice is a proactive way of dealing with and eliminating all forms of discrimination. It involves removing barriers that get in the way of accessing resources and services. This approach values and supports diversity and embraces difference when working with children, families and other stakeholders. As discussed above, the Equality Act 2010 outlines the common areas of discrimination which are protected (known as protective characteristics). However, we must also be mindful of other areas of disadvantage and discrimination such as poverty. Children and families who are living in poverty and attend your settings will have limited resources and should not be excluded from accessing activities or services as a result of their situation. This is where our focus on equality and social justice is crucial and can make a positive difference to children and families.

Brief historical and political context around social justice

You may be familiar with Sure Start local programmes and the development of Children Centres that were initially intended to support social justice for children and families in the most deprived areas. The overall initiative was to help improve children's language and thereby help prepare them for school, identify any other developmental delay and improve referral and access to services. Other support was given to parents which included offering specific programmes to improve their parenting skills. When a need was identified, a smooth referral process to access a range of integrated services and relevant multi-agency professionals was sought. Currently local authorities continue to support the most disadvantaged 2- and 3-year-olds to access free hours of childcare (depending on need and criteria) (GOV.UK, 2022a).

What should anti-discriminatory practice look like in settings?

Dickins (2014) discusses several key points which we have adapted and summarised:

1. Anti-discriminatory should be clear and visible in the settings values, principles, policies and practices.

2. The staff team should be working closely together to be proactive in identifying issues, challenges or barriers that may be evident. They should put in place policies, procedures or actions to help eliminate these.

3. Anti-discriminatory is inclusive and therefore all stakeholders (children, parents, staff) should be involved in providing solutions. Everyone should have a voice and be listened to.

4. The resources within the setting should represent society as a whole and not just the users of the setting.

5. A setting cannot be truly inclusive if anti-discriminatory practice is not part of their daily practice.

Derman-Sparks and Tous (1989, p43) make an important point in relation to children's growing identity and where they fit into society stating that, 'gradually young children begin to figure out how they are alike and how they are different from other people, and how they feel about these differences'. Anti-discriminatory practice is therefore crucial as it impacts on children's view of others as well as themselves.

Reflective task

Consider the below case study.

Case Study

Karim is 4 years old and has been attending your setting for the last 6 months. After a long settling in period, he is now well settled into the nursery. He has Downs Syndrome* and his language development is delayed. He sees a Speech and Language Therapist regularly and is making progress with his speech and language development. Using Makaton helps him to understand and express himself in the setting and at home. The setting is planning a visit to the local park to collect leaves.

*   Taking into consideration Karim's needs, how would go about planning for this visit?

*   In your journal reflect on how you will ensure this activity addresses and meets his need and demonstrates anti-discriminatory practice.

*   Ensure your planning is informed by the relevant policies and procedures.

*   Discuss your thoughts with your mentor, colleague or tutor.

* According to the National Health Service (NHS) (2023) people with Downs syndrome are born with an extra chromosome and '...will have some level of learning disability. This means they'll have a range of abilities.'

Supporting inclusive practice is everyone's responsibility similar to that of safe-guarding. In order to ensure that everyone understands, supports and adheres to implementing inclusive practice most settings have policies including a mission statement that supports practice. Here is an example:

The Gallery Nursery's Equality, Diversity and Inclusion Policy

Mission Statement

The Gallery Nursery will treat everyone equally and as an individual ensuring to protect their rights.

We will provide equality of opportunity and actively promote anti-discriminatory practice for all children, families, staff and visitors focussing on each person's individual needs.

The nursery will not tolerate any forms of discrimination based on the protected characteristics, for example, age, gender, race including colour, nationality, ethnic or national origin, religion or belief, disability, sexual orientation, gender reas-signment, pregnancy, being married or in a civil partnership.

The nursery and its staff are fully committed to supporting this policy, and if for any reason you believe that it is not being fully implemented or adhered to, please inform the Head of the setting or a member of staff.

The policy will be reviewed annually or sooner, if deemed necessary.

Reflective task

Considering the above statement, reflect on the following questions and add your own comments to support and develop the policy.

- How could this policy support more effective recruitment? E.g. identify and eliminate any forms of bias during recruitment...

- How could this policy support staff? E.g. provide diversity training...

- How could this policy support the aims of the EYFS? E.g. every child is to be encouraged and supported to participate in all activities, ensuring that the resources provided are reflective of their individual background and tailored to meets their needs...

(Continued)

(Continued)

- How could this policy support parental involvement? E.g. acknowledging differences in families and encouraging feedback and participation where appropriate...

- Which pieces of legislation (there are a few) support this policy? E.g. The Equality Act 2010

- What does settings need to do in order to promote equality, inclusion and diversity? E.g. make 'reasonable adjustments' (The Equality Act 2010).

Challenges and barriers to implementing inclusive practice

There are a number of challenges to implementing inclusive practice and many have been identified within this chapter. However, one of the main and greatest challenges is to do with attitude and the persistence of negative attitudes (Dickins, 2014). This includes the perspectives of staff and parents and other stakeholders have towards inclusion and inclusive practice which we briefly discussed earlier in the chapter. It is important that children and parents see themselves represented within the setting, hear positive discussions, and see positive images pertaining to inclusion so that everyone can feel that they belong and are welcome.

Staff must reflect on their own attitudes, biases and prejudices as these can create barriers and be detrimental to children, families and colleagues. It is easy for biases and prejudices to unwittingly slip over into discrimination. Regular training with a targeted approach, for instance examining bias and negative attitudes will help the team to reflect and identify strategies which will aid positive development. For example, this could be surrounding the use of appropriate language when referring to children and families and having a can-do attitude.

Children are very perceptive and will live out what they see, hear and feel from their environment. Therefore, positive role models within the setting as well as at home are the basic starting point in supporting inclusive practice. This is supported when 'Urie Bronfenbrenner (1979) highlighted the notion that the culture of the home, which he termed the microsystem, operates within the wider culture' (Dickins, 2014, p3). For example, it is vital that practitioners challenge discrimination by children towards other children within the setting. This may arise, when children do not want play, sit next to or hold hands with another child due to their skin colour or accent. It is important to do this in a supportive way using appropriate language relevant to the children's age and stage of development. It is the practitioner's role to promote a sense of belonging by creating welcoming environment where all children feel valued, cared for and respected as individuals.

In the following task, consider some of the challenges and barriers to inclusive practice for different stakeholders and consider how these could be overcome. Use Table 8.1 to support you with this task.

Reflective task

This task is to get you to see what inclusion looks like from a different perspective.

Role	What could you do to support inclusive practice?	What may be some of the challenges or barriers to achieving this?	How could these challenges and barriers be overcome?	What resources may be needed?
Leader/Manager of the setting				
Student/ Practitioner				
Parent				
Children				
Wider staff team				
Visitors				

Table 8.1 Supporting inclusive practice

Summary

This chapter has considered what inclusive practice is and why it is important for the well-being of children, families and staff. It gives a breakdown of relevant and common terminologies such as discrimination, anti-discriminatory or anti-bias practice, education for social justice which are crucial in understanding and supporting your work within the EY.

There are a number of reflective tasks to consider as an individual, with colleagues or as a team to help challenge inequalities and attitudes while also supporting the development of a more inclusive setting. You would have also noted relevant legislation and policies pertinent to inclusive practice.

If you are working in an environment where everyone looks similar (from the same ethnicity), comes from the same socio-economic background (particularity if they come from an advantaged background), then it is important that the setting makes even more of an effort to reflect wider society. This can be achieved by ensuring that positive images are displayed around the setting (poster/pictures) that reflect a diverse society. It could also include resources that depict or represent a wide range of cultures. If a family walks into that setting, they should feel welcomed not just by what you say but also by what they see and hear. Challenging inequalities is everyone's business.

9 Continuous professional development and next steps

Children learn to love learning through being with adults who also love to learn.

(Anning and Edwards, 2006, p145)

Why is knowledge and understanding of continuous professional development (CPD) important and how can practitioners engage in the process?

Continuous professional learning and development is seen as integral to being an Early Years practitioner. This chapter will support practitioners and students to set targets to help them plan and identify possible professional development pathways. We focus on the Early Years Educator and the Graduate Practitioner as a recent recognised pathway, and we also explore the landscape of continuous professional development opportunities more generally.

CHAPTER OVERVIEW

In this chapter we aim to help you develop your understanding of:

- Continuous Professional Development

- The historical and political context in relation to Lifelong learning and CPD

- What journaling is and its purpose

- The different pathways for further professional development.

You will find that Chapters 2, 3, 4, 7 and 8 link closely to the topics discussed within this chapter.

This chapter links to the relevant criteria for:

Early Years Educator (Department for Education and National College for Teaching and Leadership, 2019)

- 4.1 Demonstrate a good command of the English language in spoken and written form.

- 4.2 Explain the importance of continued professional development to improve own skills and Early Years (EY) practice.

- 4.3 Engage in continuing professional development and reflective practice to improve own skills, practice and subject knowledge (for example, in English, Mathematics, music, history or modern foreign languages).

Early Childhood Graduate Practitioner Competencies (Early Childhood Studies Degree Network, 2019)

- 9.3 Evidence advanced skills in utilising reflective practice alongside research, to enhance your continual professional development in Early Childhood.

- 9.5 Recognise and evidence the importance of communicating effectively orally and in writing to others.

This chapter will discuss the importance of Lifelong Learning (LLL) and Continuous Professional Development (CPD). The services and activities that are being delivered within settings are linked directly to the quality of the staff and practitioners who work within these organisations (Rodd, 2013). Therefore, both LLL and CPD should be embedded in all professional practice and academic learning, where practitioners and students are continually self-reflective and evaluative.

LLL is often a self-motivating ambition to keep educating yourself and to fulfil the desire to be constantly learning more. It involves developing new skills, updating old ones and keeping yourself relevant in a continually changing world. CPD helps you to move 'from "becoming" a professional to "being" a professional' (Basford and Hodson, 2011, p109). CPD is a terminology you may have heard being used often and refers to learning and development which students and practitioners undergo throughout their career/s. Both LLL and CPD are fluid concepts, ever developing and evolving. The Early Years Foundation Stage (EYFS) (Department for Education (DfE), 2021a, p26) state that, 'the daily experience of children in early years settings and the overall quality of provision depends on all practitioners having appropriate qualifications, training, skills, knowledge, and a clear understanding of their roles and responsibilities. Providers must ensure that all staff receive induction training to help them understand their roles and responsibilities'.

As a practitioner you have a responsibility to continually develop your knowledge and skills and also to contribute any learning to the organisation you work for. This includes supporting your colleagues, the children and families you work with to the best of your ability in all aspects of your role. The benefits of CPD are many and we have highlighted a few below:

- It helps to develop self-esteem, self-confidence and improve your practice

- Supports and enhances knowledge and understanding

- Increases skills and competence in your work with colleagues, children and families

- Helps you to be more reflective and self-aware

- It can help you prepare for dealing with complex challenges and situations

- Keeps you updated and knowledgeable in your area of work, for example, on new legislation and policies

- Helps you to identify any gaps in your knowledge and understanding for example if you were worried that a child is being abused (HM Government, 2015).

Historical and political context: Career pathways in early education and childcare

It is widely recognised that the quality of early childhood provision has a lasting impact on children's learning and development and one key determent of high quality is the qualification of practitioners. This was clearly shown by the Effective Provision of Pre-School Education (EPPE) Project which found 'children made more progress in pre-school centres where staff had higher qualifications' (Sylva et al., 2004, p4). This finding is of particular importance in light of the achievement gap between children from disadvantaged backgrounds and their more privileged peers, which is evident by the time they start compulsory schooling (Social Mobility Commission, 2020). Findings from an independent review of early education and childcare qualifications identified the need to improve EY qualifications and to 'increase graduate pedagogical leadership in all early years settings' (Nutbrown, 2012, p73). The review's recommendations aimed to professionalise and raise the status of the sector as a whole, recommending those on pathways such as the (then) Early Years Professional Status (EYPS) being able to gain EY specialist Qualified Teacher Status (QTS). Only a few of the 19 recommendations made by Nutbrown's (2012) review were implemented. Although changes were made to graduate qualifications, 'disparity in the perception and treatment of Early Years Professional/Early Years Teacher and Qualified Teacher Status (QTS) staff in the sector remains' (Pascal et al., 2020, p6). As found by the Social Mobility Commission (2020) the low pay of those working in the EY sector is evidence of the lack of status. The report shows that salaries in the sector do not reflect the complex demands placed on practitioners. Research carried out by Haux et al. (2022) was able to identify the impact of COVID-19 on EY provision. The study established that COVID-19 led to reduced demand for childcare places. It revealed government funding levels often do not match actual provider costs, which impacted negatively on many settings. Subequently, the impact of this may be felt by settings in their ability to recruit and retain highly qualified staff. In turn, this could put the government's ambition to narrow the gap in educational outcomes for the most disadvantaged children in society at risk.

The government highlights a career in EY is rewarding and full of variety, and the many possibilities open to those entering the profession is demonstrated in the EY career progression map (DfE, 2022d). Progression routes are based on achieving the Level 3 Early Years Educator (EYE) qualification. We have outlined in the introduction chapter the criteria for the EYE and Graduate Practitioner (GP) and you can find these detailed at the beginning of each of the chapters. The EY career progression map by the DfE (2022d) illustrates clearly how practitioners working in the sector can progress further. This is either through academic study, which could lead to teaching in further or higher education or work for Local Authorities. Alternatively, practitioners may specialise in an area of practice such as Special Educational Needs to become a SENCO, move into leadership roles, or attain practice competencies at graduate level and become a GP. To meet the requirements of the GP, it is explicitly outlined that practitioners need to evidence that they are able to and understand the importance of advocating for young children's rights and participation, implement inclusive practice and engage in ongoing professional development (Early Childhood Studies Degree Network, 2019). This will no doubt attract practitioners who are committed to making a positive difference to children and their families. The desire to have a positive impact on those children who are considered as being the most disadvantaged is a core value for many entering the profession.

Within Chapter 4 Leading Practice, we discuss the role and responsibilities of the leader or manager in supporting staff development. Rodd (2013) highlights the importance of supervision as it helps to develop practitioners' knowledge and skills and impacts on their professional competence in their daily practice. As discussed in Chapter 4 supervision is an opportunity for you to be self-reflective. Throughout this book, we have asked you to fully engage in points of reflection and journaling as we know this supports CPD. We emphasise with Leeson (2004, p145) that 'thinking over one's actions past and present and identifying the lessons for future actions should be a crucial aspect of professional work and lifelong learning' and integral to reflective practice.

It is important to develop this good practice, where you continually grapple with your daily experiences and modify your actions or thoughts as a result of new knowledge, understanding and learning.

What is journaling and its purpose?

Etherington (2004) believes that a reflective journal is a private document that is used to document your thoughts and feelings about any number of issues that seem important to you. Moon (2006, p1) describes it as 'vehicle for reflection'. Journaling can be a powerful tool to critically evaluate your role as it can:

- Bring together both the personal and professional; it can also support professional development

- Allow you to express your thoughts and feelings, to review and learn from them

- Prompt you into recording what you think you should do next

- Help you to problem solve

- Support you in teaching yourself through your professional practice

- 'Journals can be used to improve writing skills, improve analytical and creative thinking and build self-awareness' (Cunliffe, 2004, p418).

How then to use and keep a log of your learning if you are not experienced with the action of journaling? You could start by getting a blank exercise book and fold the page in half (long ways) or draw a line down the middle of the page. Use only the left-hand side of your journal page for recording your feelings or thoughts; try to leave the right-hand side blank. When you look at the writing at a later date or time, you can begin to ask yourself questions or look for patterns in your behaviour. These can then be recorded on the right-hand side of the page. If you choose not to keep your journal in book form, you could use perhaps a loose-leaf format. If you find it difficult to write in your journal due to being busy during the day, for example, then try sending yourself a quick email that records the main points that you do not wish to forget, then you can write it up later. If you find writing difficult, you could try using mind-maps, or other diagrams for recording your thoughts and feelings. Using different coloured highlighter pens can be useful in the evaluation and analysis of your journal. Decide on a colour for different aspects of your writing, e.g. red for team issues or blue for working with families and parents. Go through your journal highlighting extracts using your colour coding system. This will help you to identify any patterns emerging in your behaviour and your responses to situations (National College for School Leadership, n.d.).

For those of you who may have future leadership ambitions or aspirations, it is important to note that 'leadership is considered by some to be related to a particular stage of career development-that is, people with more experience are more likely to have acquired the expertise required to undertake leadership roles and responsibilities' (Rodd, 2013, p51). CPD is, therefore, essential to help you acquire the skills, knowledge and understanding to be in the best position to take on leadership roles. You can engage in LLL and access CPD in many ways, we have highlighted some of these below:

- Attending conferences

- Internal training within the local authority, for example, safeguarding, first aid, food hygiene

- External training, for example, CPD courses offered by national or local organisations

- Reading relevant journals, books, magazines such as Nursery World

- Engaging in regular supervision, mentoring or coaching programmes

- Completing a professional qualification, for example, completing a BA Hons in Early Childhood Studies with practitioner status (these could be studied part-time and through a distance learning programme).

Considering your aspirations as a professional in the EY or wider education sector is likely to take you out of your comfort zone and may make you feel overwhelmed. However, thinking of the possibilities open to you may motivate you and ignite a desire to enhance your skills, as well as your subject knowledge and understanding, both in theory and practice. Gaining a new position as a leader or manager of a setting or by having specialist training as a SENCO, you have the potential to impact and influence the experiences of the children and families in your care and this can make a positive difference. This may be an exciting prospect and will motivate you to put in place the steps necessary to achieve your goal. At the same time, you may consider and reflect on how to start the process of planning your future career or next steps.

If you have not already done so, this is a good time to fully utilise your reflective learning journal. You may record instances or experiences from your every-day life that are significant to you. Upon reflection, they may demonstrate and reveal personal and professional strengths, your specific interests and passions on the subject of early childhood education and care and your core values. In Chapter 3 on 'Working with Diverse Families and a Range of Professionals', we have explored professional skills of practitioners and values underpinning early childhood practice. You may want to remind yourself of these before engaging with the following reflective tasks.

The reflective task below aims to help you get to know yourself better. Through reflection on practice, we guide you towards identifying areas of strengths, interest and what is important to you in your professional practice. Importantly, the tasks should help with recognising areas where you could develop additional skills, knowledge and understanding. Whether you are in practice, or a student on placement, as part of LLL the tasks will be helpful in guiding you towards future professional development.

Reflective task

Reflect on your interactions with either children and families, colleagues, managers or other stakeholders

- What have you learnt about yourself and how you interact with others?

  ○ Reflect and note down your strengths and areas that need developing

  ○ Discuss your findings with your mentor, manager or tutor to get feedback on their perspective of your strengths and areas to develop.

The second reflective task aims to help you to identify specific interests and aspirations as your core values.

Reflective task

Note in your reflective learning journal which tasks and areas of provision and practice you feel most comfortable with.

- Reflect on why you feel comfortable in these areas
  - Use the reflections discussed above in mentor meetings or 1:1 meetings with the manager or leader to plan next steps for further development
- Which areas of provision and practice may you not be comfortable with at this time?
  - What areas are these and whose support could you draw on to develop additional skills, knowledge and understanding in these area(s)?

Your reflective journal can serve as an effective tool to get to know yourself better and identify where your potentials are as professional in the field of early childhood. Your reflections may direct you quite naturally to the most appropriate career pathways for you. Begin to make regular journal entries, aiming for these to be recorded weekly. You will find over time, your evidence of the skills, attributes and experience you have logged and reflected upon or demonstrated will help you to narrow down possible future roles which will match your professional qualities and skills. From there you can begin the process of planning your professional development by identifying the options and opportunities open to you. Discussing your ideas and reflections with mentors, tutors or colleagues, in particular, where they have experience in specific roles will further guide you towards the many possibilities open to you. For example, if you are considering becoming a room leader, speaking to a room leader in your setting about their experience will give you deeper insight into the role. Making a decision on the most suitable career pathway will enable you to begin to plan, so your goal becomes reality.

The range of early childhood provision differs widely, from maintained schools and nurseries to private, voluntary and independent settings (PVI) and childminders. You may wish to gain insight into what it is like to work for different types of providers, before making a firm decision on your future career goal. In addition, opportunities to gain experience in settings which follow a specific pedagogical approach and curriculum offer further professional development options. For example, you may wish to achieve a professional qualification that allows you to work or lead in a Montessori, Steiner or setting following the Froebelian approach. Professional development opportunities are available for practitioners who wish to work in settings inspired by the Reggio Emilia approach or introduce the work of Emmi Pikler into their practice. Training as a Forest School leader offers further opportunities to enhance your EY practice and we will look in detail into these opportunities in the following reflective task.

Reflective task

For this task, we ask you to research the opportunities for gaining a professional qualification or CPD in relation to pedagogical approaches that some settings may follow, and which will assist you when you apply for specific roles in a particular setting or settings that follow distinct approaches. Explore the opportunities relating to the different approaches to EY practice below. This will widen your horizons and support your knowledge and understanding of the range of experiences within the early childhood sector. Use Table 9.1 to help you with this task.

	Maria Montessori	Rudolf Steiner	Friedrich Froebel	Reggio Emilia	Emmi Pikler	Forest School
What are the key principles of the approach/ pedagogy?						
At which level can I study or train? Can I study? (the different levels relates to the Regulated Qualifications Framework (RQF). These range from entry level (level 1) to Doctorate/ PhD level (level 8) (GOV.UK, 2022c)						
What are the training or CPD courses available? (e.g. content of study)						
What are the entry requirements for the training/ course?						
Is the course/ training accredited? If yes, by whom?						
Is the qualification recognised in the United Kingdom?						

(Continued)

(Continued)

	Maria Montessori	Rudolf Steiner	Friedrich Froebel	Reggio Emilia	Emmi Pikler	Forest School
What is the duration of the course?						
Where is the training located?						
Are there opportunities for further professional qualifications/CPD?						
Are there options to study online or via distance learning?						
Contact information						
Further resources						
Further information						

Table 9.1   CPD and training opportunities relating to pedagogical approaches

Discuss your findings with other students, your mentor or tutor.

Professional development within the early childhood and education sector generally happens within the timeframe of the academic year. You may need to evidence specific practice experience or academic qualification, before being able to start on a specific programme. The use of a reflective journal will be helpful at this point, as it may prompt you to set in motion the process of thinking through potential challenges and how to address these.

Pathways for further professional development

You may already be familiar with using a Professional Development Plan (PDP), if not, it is generally an outline of what you would like to see happen or achieve in the short, medium and long-term. It relates to your professional ambitions and how you plan to go about achieving it. A PDP outlines your goals and shows what needs to be completed by you and by when. PDPs guide you into taking a step-by-step approach and assist you in planning for a particular outcome, for example, a new position or role. These plans can be a useful tool which you create at different points in your career to help you identify next steps as you progress in your professional development. In the following reflective task, we have included a sample PDP for you to begin reflecting and outlining your future professional development.

Reflective task

Use the sample PDP grid below to help you plan your next professional steps. You may want to plan for a long-term goal, for example, where you see yourself in five years' time. It may relate to a medium-term goal, that you hope to achieve within the next two years or a short-term goal to attain in the next few months or within a year.

Depending on your aspirations or ambition reflect on where you want to be professionally in the near future. It may be, for example in, the following roles or positions: Manager/Leader, Teaching Assistant, SENCO, Health Visiting Assistant, Social Work Assistant or other roles. See Table 9.2 below.

What is your professional goal or objective see example below	Identify what skills or additional qualifications are needed for this role/ position	What actions do you need to take to achieve your objective e.g. attend training, register on a specific course?	When do you expect to complete the identified actions by?	What resources or costs will be needed?	What will success look like?	What may be some of the challenges for you?
Become a Special Educational Needs Coordinator (SENCO)	1. 2. 3. 4.	1. 2. 3. 4.	1. 2. 3. 4.	1. 2. 3. 4.	1. 2. 3. 4.	1. 2. 3. 4.
Become a Teaching Assistant (TA)	1. 2. 3. 4.	1. 2. 3. 4.	1. 2. 3. 4.	1. 2. 3. 4.	1. 2. 3. 4.	1. 2. 3. 4.
Become a Manager/Leader	1. 2. 3. 4.	1. 2. 3. 4.	1. 2. 3. 4.	1. 2. 3. 4.	1. 2. 3. 4.	1. 2. 3. 4.
Become a Health Visiting Assistant	1. 2. 3. 4.	1. 2. 3. 4.	1. 2. 3. 4.	1. 2. 3. 4.	1. 2. 3. 4.	1. 2. 3. 4.
Become a Social Work Assistant	1. 2. 3. 4.	1. 2. 3. 4.	1. 2. 3. 4.	1. 2. 3. 4.	1. 2. 3. 4.	1. 2. 3. 4.

Table 9.2   Sample professional development plan

When setting personal or professional development goals, the use of SMART targets is widely recognised as being effective. The acronym SMART stands for specific, measurable, attainable, relevant and timed and relates to the goals you set yourself. Developing your goals according to these attributes will ensure that they are clear and focussed.

- **Specific**: your target clearly identifies what you wish to achieve, for example, rather than: working in a school, specify the role you wish to pursue, such as SEN support teaching assistant, Early Years Teacher or Primary Teacher.

- **Measurable**: this relates to you being able to recognise when you have achieved your goal, for example, having secured a post as SEN support teaching assistant, or holding Qualified Teacher Status (QTS).

- **Attainable**: the target you set yourself needs to be achievable for you; when setting your goal, you will need to take into account for example previous relevant qualifications, financial, personal and family circumstances and whether these will be supportive of you achieving your goal.

- **Relevant or realistic**: set your target, so you are challenged, yet not overstretched. You should feel a sense of achievement when you have reached your target. Similarly, if your target is set too low, you may begin to regret the choice made and lose motivation. Setting a realistic target requires you to know yourself and how you best learn, for example.

- **Timed**: outline a time frame which captures how long it will take until you have reached your goal. You should take account of, for example, application deadlines, having to gain a certain amount of work experience, or changes to your personal circumstances and how these will impact on your planning. This will help you to set realistic expectations and you remain motivated as you pursue your goal.

Your career choices may be further influenced by the age group of children you enjoy working with, or you may have identified that you have not gained experience of working with a specific age group and this will also inform your PDP. You may want to get support in order to complete your PDP. Speak with your manager, mentor, tutor or colleague, who may be able to assist or advise you further.

Reflective task

Having completed your PDP above, now check your plan against the SMART targets.

- Look for each of the SMART attributes in your PDP

- Reflect if any improvements are needed to the PDP

- Revise your PDP accordingly, and if you can, discuss further with your mentor, or tutor.

Summary

This chapter identifies what LLL and CPD are. It has given you a brief overview of the historical and political context and explains where LLL and CPD sit within the framework of professional qualifications in the United Kingdom. Within this chapter we have explored possible next steps and career pathway opportunities. We encouraged you to use a development plan as a way of igniting your desire to enhance your skills and knowledge. Hopefully this will motivate you to work towards achieving any future goals. Throughout the book, you have been reflecting on practice and provision and we have emphasised the value of keeping a reflective journal and its importance in relation to CPD. There are a number of tasks that allow you to begin reflecting and exploring pathways for future professional development using SMART targets. We have given you tools that will enable you to move forward more effectively and confidently with LLL and CPD.

References

Adoption and Children Act 2002, Chapter 38, available at: https://www.legislation.gov.uk/ukpga/2002/38/notes/division/4/2/10 (accessed on 3.11.22)

African Union (1990) African Charter on the Rights and Welfare of the Child, available at: https://au.int/sites/default/files/treaties/36804-treaty-african_charter_on_rights_welfare_of_the_child.pdf (accessed on 05.01.2022)

African Union (2019) African Charter on the Rights and Welfare of the Child, Treaties, Protocols and Conventions, available at: https://au.int/en/treaties/african-charter-rights-and-welfare-child (accessed on 05.01.2022)

Allen, G. (2011) Early Intervention: The Next Steps, available at: https://assets.publishing.service.gov.uk/government/uploads/system/uploads/attachment_data/file/284086/early-intervention-next-steps2.pdf (accessed on 19.12.2021)

Anning, A. and **Edwards, A.** (2006) *Promoting Children's Learning from Birth to Five: Developing the New Early Years Professional*, Maidenhead: Open University Press

Archard, D. (2015) *Children: Rights and Childhood*, London: Routledge

Aubrey, C. (2012) *Leading and Managing in the Early Years* (2nd ed.), London: SAGE

Baldock, P., Fitzgerald, D. and **Kay, J.** (2013) *Understanding Early Years Policy*, London: SAGE

Basford, J. and **Hodson, E.** (2011) *Successful Placements in Early Years Settings*, Exeter: Learning Matters

Bolton, G. (2014) *Reflective Practice, Writing and Professional Development* (4th ed.), London: SAGE

Boylan, J. and **Dalrymple, J.** (2011) 'Advocacy, Social Justice and Children's Rights', *Practice*, Vol. 23, No. 1, pp. 19–30

Bronfenbrenner, U. (1979) *The Ecology of Human Development: Experiment by Nature and Design*, London: Harvard University Press

Burr, V. (2015) *Social Constructionism* (3rd ed.), London: Routledge

Campbell-Barr, V. and **Leeson, C.** (2016) *Quality and Leadership in the Early Years: Research, Theory and Practice*, London: SAGE

Carter, C. and **Nutbrown, C.** (2014) 'The Tools of Assessment: Watching and Learning', in **Pugh, G.** and **Duffy, B.** (Eds) *Contemporary Issues in the Early Years* (6th ed.), London: SAGE

Child Poverty Act 2010, Chapter 9, available at: https://www.legislation.gov.uk/ukpga/2010/9/notes/contents (accessed on 04.05.2022)

Childcare Act 2006, Chapter 21, available at: https://www.legislation.gov.uk/ukpga/2006/21 (accessed on 02.11.2022)

Children Act 1989, Chapter 41, available at: https://www.legislation.gov.uk/ukpga/1989/41/contents (accessed on August 2022)

Children Act 2004, Chapter 31, available at: https://www.legislation.gov.uk/ukpga/2004/31/contents (accessed on 04.05.22)

Children and Families Act 2014, Chapter 6, available at: https://www.legislation.gov.uk/ukpga/2014/6/contents/enacted (accessed on 17.06.2022)

Children and Social Work Act 2017, Chapter 16, available at: https://www.legislation.gov.uk/ukpga/2017/16/contents/enacted (accessed on 05.11.2022)

Children's Rights Alliance for England (2022) Children's Rights & the Law, available at: http://www.crae.org.uk/childrens-rights-the-law/laws-protecting-childrens-rights/un-convention-on-the-rights-of-the-child/ (accessed on 05.01.2022)

Children's Workforce Development Council (2008a) Guidance to the Standards for the Award of Early Years Professional Status, available at: https://webarchive.nationalarchives.gov.uk/ukgwa/20081202141448/http://www.cwdcouncil.org.uk/eyps (accessed 02.11.2022)

Children's Workforce Development Council (2008b) Integrated Working Explained, available at: https://assets.publishing.service.gov.uk/government/uploads/system/uploads/attachment_data/file/182200/integrated_working_explained.pdf (accessed on 04.05.22)

Clark, A. (2017) *Listening to Young Children* (3rd ed.), London: Jessica Kingsley Publishers

Clark, A. and Moss, P. (2011) *Listening to Young Children: The Mosaic approach* (2nd ed.), London: National Children's Bureau

Clark, M. (1983) *Family Life and School Achievement: Why Poor Black Children Succeed or Fail*, Chicago: The University of Chicago Press

Clark, R. (2010) *Childhood in Society*, Exeter: Learning Matters

Colwell, J. (2015) *Reflective Teaching in Early Education*, London: Bloomsbury

Creasy, K. (2015) 'Defining Professionalism in Teacher Education Programs', *Journal of Education and Social Policy*, Vol. 2, No. 2, pp. 23–25

Cunliffe, A. (2004) 'On Becoming a Critically Reflexive Practitioner', *Journal of Management Education*, Vol. 28, No. 4, pp. 407–426

Data Protection Act 2018, Chapter 12, available at: https://www.legislation.gov.uk/ukpga/2018/12/contents/enacted (accessed on September 2022)

Department for Children, Schools and Families (2008) Statutory Framework for the Early Years Foundation Stage, available at: https://earlyyearsmatters.co.uk/wp-content/uploads/2011/01/Statutory-Framework-for-the-Early-Years-Foundation-Stage-EYM.pdf (accessed on 15.06.2022)

Department for Education (2010) Common Core of Skills and Knowledge for the Children's and Young People's Workforce, available at: https://www.foundationyears.org.uk/files/2015/02/Common-core.pdf (accessed on 28.04.2022)

Department for Education (2013) The National Curriculum in England, Key Stages 1 and 2 Framework Document, available at: https://assets.publishing.service.gov.uk/government/uploads/system/uploads/attachment_data/file/425601/PRIMARY_national_curriculum.pdf (accessed on 06.11.2022)

Department for Education and Timpson, E. (2013) *Written statement to Parliament, working together to safeguard children*, available at: https://www.gov.uk/government/speeches/working-together-to-safeguard-children#:~:text='Working%20Together%20to%20Safeguard%20Children'%20(2010)%2C%20the,when%20conducting%20assessments%20of%20children (accessed on 12.04.23)

Department for Education (2014) National Curriculum and Assessment from September 2014: Information for Schools, available at: https://assets.publishing.service.gov.uk/government/uploads/system/uploads/attachment_data/file/358070/NC_assessment_quals_factsheet_Sept_update.pdf (accessed on October 2022)

Department for Education (2015) What to Do if You're Worried a Child Is Being Abused, Advice for Practitioners, available at: https://assets.publishing.service.gov.uk/government/uploads/system/uploads/

attachment_data/file/419604/What_to_do_if_you_re_worried_a_child_is_being_abused.pdf (accessed on 05.05.2022)

Department for Education (2019) Check Early Years Qualifications, available at: https://www.gov.uk/guidance/early-years-qualifications-finder#early-childhood-studies-ecs-and-related-degrees (accessed on 19.12.21)

Department for Education (2021a) Statutory Framework for the Early Years Foundation Stage, available at: https://assets.publishing.service.gov.uk/government/uploads/system/uploads/attachment_data/file/974907/EYFS_framework_-_March_2021.pdf (accessed on October 2022)

Department for Education (2021b) Understanding Progress in the 2020/21 Academic Year, available at: https://assets.publishing.service.gov.uk/government/uploads/system/uploads/attachment_data/file/1062286/Understanding_progress_in_the_2020_to_2021_academic_year_Findings_from_the_summer_term_and_summary_of_all_previous_findings.pdf (accessed on October 2022)

Department for Education (2021c) Development Matters, Non-statutory Curriculum Guidance for the Early Years Foundation Stage, available at: https://assets.publishing.service.gov.uk/government/uploads/system/uploads/attachment_data/file/1007446/6.7534_DfE_Development_Matters_Report_and_illustrations_web__2_.pdf (accessed on October 2022)

Department for Education (2022a) The role of the Early Years Special Educational Needs Coordinator, available at: https://assets.publishing.service.gov.uk/government/uploads/system/uploads/attachment_data/file/1059695/The_Role_of_the_Early_Years_SENCO.pdf (accessed on 05.04.2023)

Department for Education (2022b) Keeping Children Safe in Education 2022, Statutory Guidance for Schools and Colleges, available at: https://assets.publishing.service.gov.uk/government/uploads/system/uploads/attachment_data/file/1101454/Keeping_children_safe_in_education_2022.pdf (accessed on September 2022)

Department for Education (2022c) Foundation Stage Profile, 2023 Handbook, available at: https://assets.publishing.service.gov.uk/government/uploads/system/uploads/attachment_data/file/1109972/Early_Years_Foundation_Stage_profile_2023_handbook.pdf (accessed on October 2022)

Department for Education (2022d) Early Years Career Progression Map, available at: https://www.ncfe.org.uk/media/mrxhz3m0/dfe-career-pathway-map.pdf (accessed on 06.11.2022)

Department for Education and Department of Health (2015) Special Educational Needs and Disability Code of Practice: 0 to 25 Years, available at: https://assets.publishing.service.gov.uk/government/uploads/system/uploads/attachment_data/file/398815/SEND_Code_of_Practice_January_2015.pdf (accessed on 03.11.2022)

Department for Education and National College for Teaching and Leadership (2019) Early Years Educator Level 3: Qualifications Criteria, available at: https://www.gov.uk/government/publications/early-years-educator-level-3-qualifications-criteria/early-years-educator-level-3-qualifications-criteria (accessed on 06.11.2022)

Department for Education and Skills (2001) Special Educational Needs Code of Practice, available at: https://assets.publishing.service.gov.uk/government/uploads/system/uploads/attachment_data/file/273877/special_educational_needs_code_of_practice.pdf (accessed on 05.11.2022)

Derman-Sparks, L. and **Taus, K.** (1989) 'We're different … and we're friends', *Scholastic: Children Today*, Vol. 4, No. 3, pp. 43–60

Dermott, E. and **Fowler, T.** (2021) 'What Is a Family and Why Does It Matter?', *Social Sciences*, Vol. 9, No. 5, p. 83

Desforges, C. and **Abouchaar, A.** (2003) *The Impact of Parental Involvement, Parent Support and Family Education on Pupil Achievement and Adjustment: A Literature Review*. Research Report 433, London: DfES Publications

Dickins, M. (2014) *A to Z of Inclusion in Early Childhood*, Maidenhead: Open University Press

Draper, L. and **Duffy, B.** (2006) 'Working with Parents', in **Duffy, B.** (Ed) *Contemporary Issues in the Early Years* (4th ed.), London: SAGE

Early Childhood Forum (2022) Terms of Reference, available at: http://earlychildhoodforum.org/docs/ECF_ Terms_of_Reference_v21.pdf (accessed on 05.01.2022)

Early Childhood Studies Degree Network (2019) *Early Childhood Graduate Practitioner Competencies*, available at: https://www.qaa.ac.uk/docs/qaa/sbs/sbs-early-childhood-studies-22.pdf?sfvrsn=91acdc81_2 (accessed on 11.04.2023)

Early Childhood Studies Degree Network (ECSDN) (2022) Developing Graduate and Postgraduate Level Education, Training and Research in the Field of Early Childhood Studies, available at: https://www.ecsdn.org/ (accessed on 05.11.2022)

Early Education (2021) Birth to 5 Matters: Non-statutory Guidance for the Early Years Foundation Stage, available at: https://birthto5matters.org.uk/wp-content/uploads/2021/04/Birthto5Matters-download.pdf (accessed on October 2022)

Elfer, P., Goldschmied, E. and **Selleck, D.** (2012) *Key Persons in the Early Years: Building Relationships for Quality Provision in Early Years Settings and Primary Schools*, Abingdon: Routledge

Equality Act 2010, Chapter 15, available at: https://www.legislation.gov.uk/ukpga/2010/15/contents (accessed on 04.05.22)

Equality and Human Rights Commission (2018) Understanding Equality, available at: https://www. equalityhumanrights.com/en/secondary-education-resources/useful-information/understanding-equality (accessed on 08.09.22)

Etherington, K. (2004) *Becoming a Reflexive Researcher: Using Our Selves in Research*, London and Philadelphia: Jessica Kingsley Publishers

Field, F. (2010) The Foundation Years: Preventing Poor Children Becoming Poor Adults, available at: https:// webarchive.nationalarchives.gov.uk/ukgwa/20110120090128/http://povertyreview.independent.gov.uk/ media/20254/poverty-report.pdf (accessed on 19.12.2021)

Fitzgerald, D. (2010) *Parent Partnership in the Early Years*, London: Continuum

Fitzgerald, D. and **Kay, J.** (2016) *Understanding Early Years Policy* (4th ed.), London: SAGE

Forsyth, J. (2013) Eglantyne Jebb: A True Children's Champion, available at: https://www.savethechildren. org.uk/blogs/2013/eglantyne-jebb-%2525e2%252580%252593-a-true-children%2525e2%252580% 252599s-champion (accessed on 02.11.2022)

Frost, N. (2021) *Safeguarding Children and Young People: A Guide for Professionals Working Together*, London: SAGE

Gerhardt, S. (2004) *Why Love Matters: How Affection Shapes a Baby's Brain*, London: Routledge

Giardiello, P. (2014) *Pioneers in Early Childhood Education: The Roots and Legacies of Rachel and Margaret McMillan, Maria Montessori and Susan Isaacs*, Abingdon: Routledge

Gillard, D. (2006) 1933 Hadow Report (Text), available at: http://www.educationengland.org.uk/documents/ hadow1933/hadow1933.html (accessed on 19.12.2021)

Gillard, D. (2014) *Children Act 1948, Chapter 43*, available at: http://www.educationengland.org.uk/ documents/acts/1948-children-act.html

Gillard, D. (2004) The Plowden Report (1967), Children and their Primary Schools, available at: http://www.educationengland.org.uk/documents/plowden/plowden1967-1.html (accessed on 05.05.2022)

GOV.UK (2003) The Victoria Climbie Inquiry: Report of an Inquiry by Lord Laming, available at: https://www.gov.uk/government/publications/the-victoria-climbie-inquiry-report-of-an-inquiry-by-lord-laming (accessed on 05.11.2022)

GOV.UK (2014) National Professional Qualification for Headship (NPQH), available at: https://www.gov.uk/guidance/national-professional-qualification-for-headship-npqh (accessed on 05.11.2022)

GOV.UK (2022a) Free Education and Childcare for 2-Year-Olds, available at: https://www.gov.uk/help-with-childcare-costs/free-childcare-2-year-olds (accessed on 08.09.22)

GOV.UK (2022b) Check Someone's Criminal Record as an Employer, Early Childhood Studies Degree Network, 2019, available at: https://www.gov.uk/dbs-check-applicant-criminal-record (accessed on October 2022)

GOV.UK (2022c) What Qualification Levels Mean, https://www.gov.uk/what-different-qualification-levels-mean/list-of-qualification-levels (accessed on October 2022)

Government Equalities Office (2010) Equality Act 2010: What Do I Need to Know? A Summary Guide for Public Sector Organisations, available at: https://assets.publishing.service.gov.uk/government/uploads/system/uploads/attachment_data/file/85021/public-sector.pdf (accessed on 25.08.22)

Grenier, J. (2020) EYFS Guidance: Effective Practice, Part1 -Starting Points, available at: https://www.nurseryworld.co.uk/features/article/eyfs-guidance-effective-practice-part-1-starting-points (accessed on 27.10.21)

Hargreaves, E., Gipps, C. and Pickering, A. (2018) 'Assessment for Learning', in Cremin, T. and Burnett, C. (Eds) Learning to Teach in the Primary School, Abingdon: Routledge

Haux, T., Butt, S., Rezaian, M., Garwood, E., Woodbridge, H., Bhatti, S., Woods Rogan, R. and Paul, G. (2022) The Early Years Workforce: Recruitment, Retention, and Business Planning, available at: https://assets.publishing.service.gov.uk/government/uploads/system/uploads/attachment_data/file/1072062/SCEYP_thematic_report-_April_2022.pdf (accessed on 30.10.2022)

Health and Safety Executive (2022) Health and Safety at Work etc Act 1974, available at: https://www.hse.gov.uk/legislation/hswa.htm (accessed on 05.11.2022)

Heathwood, C. (2021) Happiness and Wellbeing, Cambridge: Cambridge University Press

Hendrick, H. (2012) Children, Childhood and English Society, 1880-1990, Cambridge: Cambridge University Press

HM Government (2004) Every Child Matters: Change for Children, available at: http://www.educationengland.org.uk/documents/pdfs/2004-ecm-change-for-children.pdf (accessed on 05.11.2022)

HM Government (2015) What to Do if You're Worried a Child Is Being Abused, Advice for Practitioners, available at: https://assets.publishing.service.gov.uk/government/uploads/system/uploads/attachment_data/file/419604/What_to_do_if_you_re_worried_a_child_is_being_abused.pdf (accessed on 22.01.2022)

HM Government (2018a) Working Together to Safeguard Children, A Guide to Inter-agency Working to Safeguard and Promote the Welfare of Children, available at: https://assets.publishing.service.gov.uk/government/uploads/system/uploads/attachment_data/file/942454/Working_together_to_safeguard_children_inter_agency_guidance.pdf (accessed on July 2022)

HM Government (2018b) Information Sharing, Advice for Practitioners Providing Safeguarding Services to Children, Young People, Parents and Carers, available at: https://assets.publishing.service.gov.uk/government/uploads/system/uploads/attachment_data/file/1062969/Information_sharing_advice_practitioners_safeguarding_services.pdf (accessed on September 2022)

HM Treasury, Department for Education and Skills, Department for Work and Pensions and Department for Trade and Industry (2004) Choice for Parents, the Best Start for Children: A Ten Year Strategy for Childcare, available at: https://dera.ioe.ac.uk/5274/2/02_12_04__pbr04childcare_480-1.pdf (accessed on 05.11.2022)

Holmes, J. (2014) *John Bowlby and Attachment Theory*, London: Routledge

Horwath, J. and Platt, D. (2019) *The Child's World: The Essential Guide to Assessing Vulnerable Children, Young People and Their Families* (3rd ed.), London: Jessica Kingsley Publishers

Howard, S. and Hutchinson, A. (2021) 'Assessment', in Palaiologou, I. (Ed.) *The Early Years Foundation Stage: Theory and Practice*, London: SAGE

Independent Commission on Good Governance on Good Governance in Public Services (the Langlands Commission) (2005) *Good Governance Standards for Public Services*, London: CIPFA, OPM & Joseph Rowntree Foundation

James, A. and Prout, A. (2015) *Constructing and Reconstructing Childhood*, Abingdon: Routledge

Jarvis, P. and Liebovich, B. (2015) 'British Nurseries, Head and Heart: McMillan, Owen and the Genesis of the Education/Care Dichotomy', *Women's History Review*, Vol. 24, No. 6, pp. 917–937

John, K. (2019) 'Introduction', in Whalley, M., John, K., Whitaker, P., Klavins, E., Parker, C. and Vaggers, J. (Eds) *Democratising Leadership in the Early Years: A Systemic Approach*, Abingdon: Routledge

Jones, P. (2011) 'What Are Children's Rights? Contemporary Developments and Debates', in Jones and Walker (Eds) *Children's Rights in Practice*, London: SAGE

Jones, P. and Welch, S. (2018) *Rethinking Children's Rights* (2nd ed.), London: Bloomsbury

Kitto, E. and Bullogh, L. (2021) 'Reflective Practice', in Palaiologou, I. (Ed.) *The Early Years Foundation Stage, Theory and Practice* (4th ed.), London: SAGE

Kolb, D. (1984) *Experiential Learning: Experience as the Source of Learning and Development*, London: Prentice Hall International

Koren, M. (2004) Empowering Children: Rights-Based Library Services, available at: http://archive.ifla.org/IV/ifla70/papers/004e-Koren.pdf (accessed on 05.01.2022)

Kouzes, J. and Posner, B. (2017) *The Leadership Challenge: How to Make Extraordinary Things Happen in Organizations*, New Jersey: Wiley

Labour Party (1997) *New Labour Because Britain Deserves Better*. London: Labour Party Publications

Lane, J. (2008) *Young Children and Racial Justice*, London: National Children's Bureau

Leeson, C. (2004) 'In Praise of Reflective Practice', in Willan, J., Parker-Rees, R. and Savage, J. (Eds) *Early Childhood Studies: An Introduction to the Study of Children's Worlds and Children's Lives*, Exeter: Learning Matters Ltd

Leeson, C. (2019) 'Learning Through Placements', in Fitzgerald, D. and Maconochie, H. (Eds) *Early Childhood Studies, A Student's Guide*, London: SAGE

Lumsdon, E. (2016) *Child Protection the Early Years – A Practical Guide*, London: Jessica Kingsley Publishers

Mac Naughton, G., Hughes, P., Lawrence, H., Campbell, H. and Page, J. (2003) 'Reflecting on Contexts', in MacNaughton, G. (Ed.) *Shaping Early Childhood*, Maidenhead: Open University Press

Malaguzzi, L. (1996) 'The Right to Environment', in Filippini, T. and Vecci, V. (Eds) *The Hundred Languages of Children: The Exhibit*, Reggio Emilia: Reggio Children

Malaguzzi, L. (2011) 'No Way. The Hundred is There', in **Edwards, C., Gandini, L.** and **Forman, G.** (Eds) *The Hundred Languages of Children: The Reggio Emilia Experience in Transformation* (3rd ed.), Oxford: Praeger

Male, T. and **Ince, A.** (2021) 'Leadership', in **Palailogou, I.** (Ed.) *The Early Years Foundation Stage, Theory and Practice*, London: SAGE

Mandela, N. (1994) *Long Walk to Freedom*, London: Abacus

Maslow, A. (1943) 'A Theory of Human Motivation', *Psychological Review*, Vol. 50, No. 4, pp. 370–396

Mathers, S., Roberts, F. and **Sylva, K.** (2014) 'Quality in Early Childhood Education', in **Pugh, G.** and **Duffy, B.** (Eds) *Contemporary Issues in the Early Years* (6th ed.), London: SAGE

McIntosh, J. (2015) Final Report of the Commission on Assessment Without Levels, available at: https://assets.publishing.service.gov.uk/government/uploads/system/uploads/attachment_data/file/483058/Commission_on_Assessment_Without_Levels_-_report.pdf (accessed on October 2022)

McMahon, S. and **Watson, L.** (2019) 'Observation, Assessment and the Planning Cycle', in **McEvoy, J.** and **McMahon, S.** (Eds) *Child Centred Planning in the Early Years Foundation Stage*, London: SAGE

McMillan, M. (1919) *The Nursery School*, London: J.M. Dent and Sons Ltd

Melhuish, E., Sylva, C., Sammons, P., Siraj-Blatchford, I., and **Taggart, B.** (2001) *Social Behavioural and Cognitive Development at 3-4 Years in Relation to Family Background. The Effective Provision of Pre-school Education, EPPE Project* (Technical paper 7), London: The Institute of Education

Miller, L. and **Hevey, D.** (2012) *Policy Issues in the Early Years*, London: SAGE

Ministry of Education (2017) Te Whariki Early Childhood Curriculum, available at: https://www.education.govt.nz/assets/Documents/Early-Childhood/ELS-Te-Whariki-Early-Childhood-Curriculum-ENG-Web.pdf (accessed on October 2022)

Moon, J. (2006) *Learning Journals: A Handbook for Reflective Practice and Professional Development* (2nd ed.), Oxon and New York: Routledge

Moon, J. (2013) *Reflection in Learning and Professional Development*, Oxon: Routledge Falmer

Moore, J. (2018) *The ABC of Child Protection*, Abingdon: Routledge

Moss, P. (2003) 'Getting Beyond Childcare: Reflections on Recent Policy and Future Possibilities', in **Brannen, J.** and **Moss, P.** (Eds) *Rethinking Children's Care*, Buckingham: Open University Press

Moyles, J. (2006) *Effective Leadership and Management in the Early Years*, Maidenhead: Open University Press

Munro, E. (2011) The Munro Review of Child Protection: Final Report, A Child-Centred System, available at: https://assets.publishing.service.gov.uk/government/uploads/system/uploads/attachment_data/file/175391/Munro-Review.pdf (accessed on 05.11.2022)

National College for School Leadership (no date) *Realising Leadership: Children's centre Leaders in Action*, available at: https://dera.ioe.ac.uk/2059/1/download%3Fid%3D17344%26filename%3Drealising-leadership-childrens-centre-leaders-in-action.pdf (accessed on 05.04.2023)

National College for Teaching and Leadership (2013) *Teachers' Standards (Early Years)*, available at: https://assets.publishing.service.gov.uk/government/uploads/system/uploads/attachment_data/file/211646/Early_Years_Teachers__Standards.pdf

National Health Service (2022a) Health A – Z, available at: https://www.nhs.uk/conditions/cerebral-palsy/ (accessed on 05.01.2022)

National Health Service (2022b) Your Baby's Health and Development Reviews, available at: https://www.nhs.uk/conditions/baby/babys-development/height-weight-and-reviews/baby-reviews/ (accessed on 17.06.2022)

National Health Service (2023) Health A – Z, available at: https://www.nhs.uk/conditions/downs-syndrome/ (accessed on 25.03.2023)

Naughton, A. (2018) 'Assessing the Developmental Needs of Children and Young People', in **Horwath, J.** and **Platt, D.** (Eds) *The Child's World: The Essential Guide to Assessing Vulnerable Children, Young People and Their Families*, London: Jessica Kingsley Publishers

NSPCC (2019) Helping Adults Respond to Children Disclosing Abuse, available at: https://learning.nspcc.org.uk/research-resources/2019/let-children-know-you-re-listening (accessed on August 2022)

NSPCC (2022a) Safeguarding Children and Child Protection, available at: https://learning.nspcc.org.uk/safeguarding-child-protection#:~:text=Child%20protection%20is%20part%20of,to%20concerns%20about%20a%20child (accessed on August 2022)

NSPCC (2022b) Child Protection Definitions, available at: https://learning.nspcc.org.uk/child-protection-system/child-protection-definitions (accessed on August 2022)

NSPCC (2022c) Effects of Child Abuse, available at: https://www.nspcc.org.uk/what-is-child-abuse/effects-of-child-abuse/(accessed on August 2022)

NSPCC (2022d) Non-recent Abuse, available at: https://www.nspcc.org.uk/what-is-child-abuse/types-of-abuse/non-recent-abuse/#brain (accessed on August 2022)

NSPCC (2022e) History of Child Protection in the UK, available at: https://learning.nspcc.org.uk/child-protection-system/history-of-child-protection-in-the-uk (accessed on August 2022)

Nursery and Childminder Regulation Act 1948, Chapter 53, available at: https://www.legislation.gov.uk/ukpga/Geo6/11-12/53/enacted#:~:text=1948%20CHAPTER%2053,%5B30th%20July%201948.%5D (accessed on 05.11.2022)

Nursery World (2001) A Parent's Guide to the National Childcare Strategy, available at: https://www.nurseryworld.co.uk/news/article/a-parent-s-guide-to-the-national-childcare-strategy (accessed on 05.11.2022)

Nutbrown, C. (2012) Foundation for Quality, The Independent Review of Early Education and Childcare Qualifications, Final Report, available at: https://assets.publishing.service.gov.uk/government/uploads/system/uploads/attachment_data/file/175463/Nutbrown-Review.pdf (accessed on 06.11.2022)

Nutbrown, C., **Clough, P.** and **Atherton, F.** (2013) *Inclusion in the Early Years*, London: SAGE

Ofsted (2005) *Removing Barriers a 'Can-Do' Approach,* London: Crown Copyright London

Ofsted (2019a) Early Years Inspection Handbook for Ofsted Registered Provision, available at: https://assets.publishing.service.gov.uk/government/uploads/system/uploads/attachment_data/file/828465/Early_years_inspection_handbook.pdf (accessed on 21.03.2020)

Ofsted (2019b) Education Inspection Framework Equality, Diversity and Inclusion Statement, available at: https://assets.publishing.service.gov.uk/government/uploads/system/uploads/attachment_data/file/821069/Education_inspection_framework_-_equality__diversity_and_inclusion_statement.pdf (accessed on 08.09.22)

Ofsted (2022a) Inspecting Safeguarding in Early Years, Education and Skills, available at: https://www.gov.uk/government/publications/inspecting-safeguarding-in-early-years-education-and-skills/inspecting-safeguarding-in-early-years-education-and-skills (accessed on September 2022)

Ofsted (2022b) Childcare: Significant Events to Notify Ofsted about, available at: https://www.gov.uk/guidance/childcare-significant-events-to-notify-ofsted-about#examples-of-significant-events (accessed on September 2022)

Osgood, J. (2012) *Narratives from the Nursery: Negotiating Professional Identities in Early Childhood*, London: Routledge

Palaiologou, I. (2021) 'Preface', in **Palaiologou, I.** (Ed.) *The Early Years Foundation Stage: Theory and Practice*, London: SAGE

Papatheodorou, T. (2009) 'Exploring Relational Pedagogy', in **Papatheodorou, T.** and **Moyles, J.** (Eds) *Learning Together in the Early Years: Exploring Relational Pedagogy*, Abingdon: Routledge

Pascal, C., Bertram, T. and **Cole-Albäck, A.** (2020) Early Years Workforce Review, Revisiting the Nutbrown Review - Policy and Impact, available at: https://www.suttontrust.com/wp-content/uploads/2020/08/Early_Years_Workforce_Review_.pdf (accessed on 06.11.2022)

Qualifications and Curriculum Authority (2000) *Curriculum Guidance for the Foundation Stage*, London: Qualifications and Curriculum Authority

Quality Assurance Agency for Higher Education (2022) Subject Benchmark Statement Early Childhood Studies, available at: https://www.qaa.ac.uk/quality-code/subject-benchmark-statements/early-childhood-studies (accessed on 02.11.2022)

Rawding, S. (2019) 'Creativity, Curiosity and Resilience', in **Fitzgerald, D.** and **Maconochie, H.** (Eds) *Early Childhood Studies, A Student's Guide*, London: SAGE

Rights of Women (2014) Children and the Law: Parental Responsibility, available at: https://rightsofwomen.org.uk/wp-content/uploads/2014/10/PDF-guide-to-Children-and-the-law-parental-responsibility.pdf (accessed on 22. 01.2022)

Rinaldi, C. (2021) *In Dialogue with Reggio Emilia* (2nd ed.), London: Routledge

Robins, R. and **Callan, S.** (2009) *Managing Early Years Settings*, London: SAGE

Rodd, J. (2006) *Leadership in Early Childhood*, London: Allen & Unwin

Rodd, J. (2013) *Leadership in Early Childhood*, Maidenhead: Open University Press

Save the Children (2016) Understanding Four Most Important Sets of Children's Rights, available at: https://www.savethechildren.in/child-protection/understanding-four-most-important-sets-of-childrens-rights/ (accessed on 05.01.2022)

Shemmings, D. and **Shemmings, Y.** (2019) 'Emotional and Behavioural Development', in **Horwath, J.** and **Platt, D.** (Eds) *The Child's World: The Essential Guide to Assessing Vulnerable Children, Young People and Their Families*, London: Jessica Kingsley Publishers

Scottish Government (2014) Children's Advocacy Guidance, available at: https://www.gov.scot/publications/childrens-advocacy-guidance/#introduction-to-children-s-advocacy (accessed on 19.01.2022)

Shribman, S. and **Billingham, K.** (2009) Healthy Child Programme- Pregnancy and the First 5 Years, available at: https://assets.publishing.service.gov.uk/government/uploads/system/uploads/attachment_data/file/167998/Health_Child_Programme.pdf (accessed on 04.05.22)

Simpson, G. and **Connor, S.** (2011) *Social Policy for Social Welfare Professionals: Tools for Understanding, Analysis and Engagement*, Bristol: The Policy Press

Siraj-Blatchford, I., Sylva, K., Muttock, S., Gilden, R. and **Bel, D.** (2002) Researching Effective Pedagogy in the Early Years, available at: http://www.327matters.org/docs/rr356.pdf (accessed on 05.01.2022)

Social Mobility Commission (2020) The Stability of the Early Years Workforce in England, available at: https://assets.publishing.service.gov.uk/government/uploads/system/uploads/attachment_data/file/906906/The_stability_of_the_early_years_workforce_in_England.pdf (accessed on October 2022)

Spencer, B. and Dubiel, J. (2014) 'Inspecting and Evaluating the Quality and Standards of Early Years and Childcare Provision', in Pugh, G. and Duffy, B. (Eds) *Contemporary Issues in the Early Years* (6th ed.), London: SAGE

Standards and Testing Agency (2020a) Key Stage 1, Pre-key Stage 1: Pupils Working below the National Curriculum Assessment Standard, available at: https://assets.publishing.service.gov.uk/government/uploads/system/uploads/attachment_data/file/1109303/2021_Pre-key_stage_1_-_pupils_working_below_the_national_curriculum_assessment_standard.pdf (accessed on 06.11.2022)

Standards and Testing Agency (2020b) The Engagement Model, Guidance for Maintained Schools, Academies (Including Free Schools) and Local Authorities, available at: https://assets.publishing.service.gov.uk/government/uploads/system/uploads/attachment_data/file/903458/Engagement_Model_Guidance_2020.pdf (accessed on 06.11.2022)

Standards and Testing Agency (2021) Key Stage 1 Assessment and Reporting Arrangements, available at: https://assets.publishing.service.gov.uk/government/uploads/system/uploads/attachment_data/file/1031077/2022_Key_stage_1_assessment_and_reporting_arrangements.pdf (accessed on October 2022)

Standards and Testing Agency (2022) Key stage 1 teacher assessment guidance 2022-23, available at: https://www.gov.uk/government/publications/key-stage-1-teacher-assessment-guidance/key-stage-1-teacher-assessment-guidance (accessed on October 2022)

Sylva, K., Melhuish, E., Sammons, P., Siraj-Blatchford, I. and Taggart, B. (2004) The Effective Provision of Pre-school (EPPE) Project: Findings from Preschool to End of Key Stage 1, available at: https://dera.ioe.ac.uk/8543/7/SSU-SF-2004-01.pdf (accessed on 05.01.2022)

The Child Safeguarding Practice Review Panel (2022) *Child Protection in England, National Review into the Murders of Arthur Labinjo-Hughes and Star Hobson*, available at: https://assets.publishing.service.gov.uk/government/uploads/system/uploads/attachment_data/file/1078488/ALH_SH_National_Review_26-5-22.pdf (accessed on 12.04.2023)

The Stationery Office (2003) Every Child Matters, available at: https://assets.publishing.service.gov.uk/government/uploads/system/uploads/attachment_data/file/272064/5860.pdf (accessed on 05.11.2022)

UK Parliament (2015) Human Rights Joint Committee – Eighth Report, The UK's Compliance with the UN Convention on the Rights of the Child – Human Rights Joint Committee, available at: https://publications.parliament.uk/pa/jt201415/jtselect/jtrights/144/14404.htm (accessed on 05.01.2022)

UK Parliament (2021) Committees, Urgent Action Needed to Tackle Deep Rooted and Persistent Racial Disparities in Policing, available at: https://committees.parliament.uk/work/347/the-macpherson-report-twentytwo-years-on/news/157006/urgent-action-needed-to-tackle-deep-rooted-and-persistent-racial-disparities-in-policing#:~:text=By%202020%20BME%20officers%20represented,inspector%20are%20from%20BME%20backgrounds (accessed on 06.11.2022)

UK Parliament (2022a) *The 1833 Factory Act*, available at: https://www.parliament.uk/about/living-heritage/transformingsociety/livinglearning/19thcentury/overview/factoryact/ (accessed on 12.04.2023)

UK Parliament (2022b) The 1870 Education Act, available at: https://www.parliament.uk/about/living-heritage/transformingsociety/livinglearning/school/overview/1870educationact/ (accessed on 05.11.2022)

UNICEF (1989) The United Nations Convention on the Rights of the Child, available at: https://downloads.unicef.org.uk/wp-content/uploads/2016/08/unicef-convention-rights-child-uncrc.pdf (accessed on September 2022)

UNICEF (2010) *Advocacy Toolkit: A Guide to Influence Decisions that Improve Children's Lives*, New York: UNICEF

UNICEF (2022) What Is the UN Convention on Children's Rights?, available at: https://www.unicef.org.uk/what-we-do/un-convention-child-rights/ (accessed on 19.01.2022)

United Nations (2022) Universal Declaration of Human Rights, available at: https://www.un.org/en/about-us/universal-declaration-of-human-rights (accessed on 05.01.2022)

Walker, G. (2011) 'Children's Rights: Social Justice and Exclusion', in **Jones** and **Walker** (Eds) *Children's Rights in Practice*, London: SAGE

Walley, M. (2008) *Leading Practice in Early Years Settings*, Exeter: Learning Matters

Wells, K. (2015) *Childhood in a Global Perspective*, Cambridge: Polity Press

Western, S. (2008) *Leadership: A Critical Text*, London: SAGE

Woodhead, M. (2005) 'Early Childhood Development: A Question of Rights', *International Journal of Early Childhood*, Vol. 37, No. 3, pp. 79–98

Woodhead, M. (2015) 'Psychology and the Cultural Construction of Children's Needs', in **Prout, A.** and **James A.** (Eds.) *Constructing and Reconstructing Childhood (Classic Edition)*, London: Routledge

Yates, E. with **Appleby, M.** (2014) 'The Emerging Practitioner', in **Oates, R.** and **Hay, C.** (Eds) *The Student Practitioner in Early Childhood Studies*, Abingdon: Routledge

Young Minds and NHS England (2018) Addressing Adversity: Prioritising Adversity and Trauma-Informed Care for Children and Young People in England, available at: https://www.youngminds.org.uk/media/cmtffcce/ym-addressing-adversity-book-web-2.pdf (accessed on 06.11.2022)

Young-Ihm, K. (2002) 'Changing Curriculum for Early Childhood in England', *Early Childhood Research & Practice*, Vol. 4, No. 2

Index